Christian Faith and Public Policy
No Grounds for Divorce

ARTHUR SIMON

William B. Eerdmans Publishing Company
Grand Rapids, Michigan

To my wife, Rosamund, with love

All royalties from the sale of this book go to the Bread for the World Educational Fund

Library of Congress Cataloging-in-Publication Data

Simon, Arthur R.
  Christian faith/public policy.

  1. Church and social problems—United States—Case
studies. 2. Social action—United States—Case studies.
3. Christian ethics—United States—Case studies.
I. Title.
HN31.S546   1987   261.8'3   87-9297

ISBN 0-8028-0282-6

Contents

Acknowledgments

I want to thank the following people for reading an initial draft of this book and offering comments that were exceptionally helpful: David Beckmann; William J. Byron, S.J.; Robert P. Dugan, Jr.; James M. Dunn; James Finn; Paul Goetting; Paul Jersild; Eugene W. Linse; Charles Lutz; Theodore Malloch; Stephen V. Monsma; Ronald Pasquariello; Albert H. Quie; Harold Remus; Paul Simon; and James W. Skillen.

Dolly Youssef, my administrative assistant, deserves a special word of gratitude for typing and retyping these pages many times and for organizing her work and mine so well.

Ginger Hooven, former deputy director of Bread for the World, filled my shoes as well as hers with great skill during my five-month sabbatical, which gave me opportunity to read and write.

Other staff members of Bread for the World contributed directly and indirectly in ways too numerous to list.

My wife, Rosamund, contributed the indispensable gifts of patience and understanding, for which I am especially grateful.

My biggest debt of all is to BFW members across the land who, as they struggled for better policy responses to hunger, kept prodding me for answers to some of the questions considered in this book. They also have shared willingly their own insights and practical experience and, along with staff and board members, have been a constant source of encouragement. The flaws herein are mine, but in a real sense this book is theirs.

Arthur Simon
July 1986

Preface
Why This Book?

Christians have dual citizenship. We are citizens of God's kingdom and citizens of an earthly country. That may sound abstract and academic, but it is not. It touches on our purpose in life and the way we plan and conduct our lives. It has an immediate bearing on each one of us every day—what happens to us, what we decide to do, and how we feel about what we do. Our dual citizenship is, therefore, a powerful, life-shaping reality.

I address this situation with a particular focus in mind. I serve as the executive director of Bread for the World, a Christian citizens' movement against hunger. Since it began in 1974, Bread for the World has demonstrated—with evidence that mounts every year—that committed individuals can offer life and opportunity to others by making an impact on national policy. The evidence is striking and impressive. But wherever I go, in every part of the country, one question seldom fails to arise: "How can I get others in my congregation to understand that efforts to change public policy on hunger are important for Christians?" Often the issue is not whether such efforts are important, but whether they are even legitimate for Christians.

I have written this book in response to that question and a cluster of related concerns. For many Christians—perhaps most of them—the advocating of policy change is either unimportant or wrongheaded. It may seem hopelessly complex, hazardous, or out of place. People in the pews usually do not see a clear connection between faith and public policy, and they are nervous about making that connection. "I'd rather not get involved," they say in a variety of ways—mostly by not getting involved.

Their nervousness is understandable, because the issues *are* complex, and history is littered with examples of misguided efforts to move from faith to politics and vice versa. So I approach the question with respect for those who are not persuaded and for the fact that the road we have to walk may sometimes resemble a minefield. Yet a full celebration of faith and our ability to make our lives count for others are overriding considerations. Although we run the risk of making mistakes, we do well to remember that the biggest mistake of all is to take no risks for others—not exactly the kind of life that followers of Jesus should aspire to. We are free to fail. We are not free to do nothing.

When is it appropriate for an individual Christian, or a congregation, or a national church body to advocate government action? And how can they best do so?

In approaching such questions I draw primarily on my own experience and that of Bread for the World. So, while this book deals with principles that apply to many issues, the issue of hunger serves as its major point of reference.

I have tried to write a practical guide for people who want their lives to make a difference, not a book of theory for armchair analysts. Put another way, I have written this book to encourage Christians to let their faith be more active in love and to provide a better foundation for such action. In doing so I have left many trails unexplored. But because I have stuck to a few main paths, readers will, I hope, get a sense of direction. The questions that trouble and often impede Christians are like obstacles on a road. If we can remove them and avoid the main potholes, we may be able to get somewhere. Effective action is important because throughout the world millions of lives are in jeopardy; but one person's response—your response, to be specific—can make a difference, a difference that matters much to God.

I don't expect readers to agree with every point or emphasis of mine. Each of us brings to this discussion a special experience of faith and life. Thank God! For that reason we need to respect those with views that differ from our own. Doing so includes listening to and learning from one another with patience, aware that each of us possesses far less than perfect clarity on these matters. "Now I know in part," the apostle Paul said. That's humbling, but Paul didn't offer it as an excuse for inaction or for not trying to understand more fully. Quite the contrary. The gift of salvation that transformed and empowered Paul to offer his life in service to Christ is the same grace that transforms and empowers us. If we are to live our lives to the praise of his glory, then every part of life, including our earthly citizenship, must be placed at God's disposal.

Chapter 1
The Case for Citizen Action

*The old monk wove a basket one day; the next day he un-
wove it. The basket itself did not matter; but the weaving
and unweaving of it served as a means of spending an in-
terval, necessary to the frail human spirit, between periods
of performance of the only task that did matter, the contem-
plation of heavenly things. Only the making of a soul was
the true human value. For the rest, what did it matter whether
one wove baskets or wrought whole civilizations?*

    —John Courtney Murray, S.J., *We Hold These Truths*

*So long as Christ and the world are conceived as two op-
posing and mutually repellent spheres, man will be left in
the following dilemma: he abandons reality as a whole, and
places himself in one or other of the two spheres. He seeks
Christ without the world, or he seeks the world without Christ.*

    —Dietrich Bonhoeffer, *Ethics*

*Christians, above all others, should be concerned with social
problems and social injustices.*

    —Billy Graham

It was the evening of election day. My brother Paul and I and
a few friends walked into my parents' home in Highland, Illinois, for a late dinner and gave them the bad news: We had lost
the election.

I was a student at Concordia Seminary in St. Louis, my brother
the editor of a small-town weekly newspaper in nearby Troy.
Several months earlier, Paul had announced himself as a can-
didate for the State House of Representatives in Illinois, an an-
nouncement he made against the advice of political leaders. I
remember going along with Paul when he went to tell the county
chairman of his party that he planned to enter the race. Kenny

Ogle was a fat, friendly, cigar-chomping character who listened intently to Paul.

"Do you have any money?" he asked.

"No," replied Paul.

"Do you have an organization?"

"No," said Paul.

"Then don't run. You'll only hurt yourself."

His advice hardly surprised us. Madison County, Illinois, just across the river from St. Louis, was controlled by a strong, well-financed political machine. The machine was fueled and oiled by its connection with illegal gambling and other vice that flourished in the county. Paul had, through the unlikely instrument of his weekly newspaper, published front-page accounts of corruption in the county, giving locations and describing illegal activities with the same attentive detail that he used in reporting local weddings. He sent copies of his articles to the sheriff by registered mail with letters asking him to enforce the law, but got no replies. Finally he called for a grand jury to indict the sheriff, and he asked the Illinois Bar Association to disbar the state's attorney, who was failing to prosecute offenders.

Neither action fully succeeded, nor did either endear Paul to the Democratic leaders in Madison County. So Paul launched his campaign for state representative as an outsider in what was regarded, even by newspapers that supported him, as a losing cause. Lacking money and organizational support, he recruited volunteers. On Saturdays Paul rounded up friends, and I would bring a carload or two of seminary students. By election time we had gone door-to-door throughout the district, and Paul had shaken hands with potential voters in just about every factory, store, laundromat, and bowling alley. We sensed a warm response, even enthusiasm. We counted on another factor: In this election *two* candidates would be nominated by each party, so Paul could come in second and still win. In short, we thought we had a chance.

Then came election day. Paul and I and our volunteers spread out in pairs to work in the areas where the voting was expected to be heaviest. What Paul and I saw stunned us. At six o'clock in the morning, when the polls opened, the streets were alive with people. Hired party workers were everywhere—lined up near the polls, walking the streets, bringing in carloads of voters.

All were passing out the same sample ballots marked for the incumbents and against Paul. I remember that during the course of the day I met many organizational workers who said they were for Paul—but they all carried the same sample ballots marked for Paul's opponents. We groaned.

When we assembled late in the afternoon to compare notes, the stories of our volunteers were carbon copies of our own. Our optimism during the campaign clearly did not square with the awesome ability of the machine to muster and influence voters. So we went home and told our parents that Paul had almost certainly been defeated.

A few hours later, a group of sober-faced supporters gathered at a hall in Troy to await the returns. Soon the phones began to ring. Unbelievably, precinct after precinct called in to report results that placed Paul far ahead of both incumbents, who spent the night wondering which of them had lost. Paul had won the nomination after all.

That election launched Paul in a career of public service that ultimately led to the U.S. Senate. I tell the story for two reasons. First, it illustrates one important aspect of citizenship that I do not directly deal with in this book: participation in electoral politics. Second, it helps to explain my own journey in seeing citizenship as an opportunity for Christian service.

Of course, my journey did not begin there; it started with my parents. They served first as missionaries in China. Later my father became a parish pastor in Eugene, Oregon, where Paul and I were born. While serving as pastor my father developed a specialty in child rearing and subsequently concentrated on editing and publishing materials about Christian family life. He had a great love for people. He had a saying that reflected the childhood he spent on a Wisconsin farm: "Even the cows should be able to tell you're a Christian by the way you treat them." My father spoke out in protest during World War II when U.S. citizens of Japanese descent were rounded up on the West Coast and imprisoned in detention centers without a shred of evidence, ever, of any subversive activity. Guided by such examples, Paul and I grew up believing that faith embraced the whole of life and that all Christians—not just pastors and professional church employees—were called to full-time Christian service, no matter what their occupations. We saw faith as something that also touched matters of public life. If Christ is Lord, how could it be otherwise?

With his avid interest in current events, Paul decided while still in grade school that when he grew up he wanted to buy a weekly newspaper and go into politics, and he never changed his mind. I shifted vocational interest several times before deciding to enter the parish ministry. I remember agonizing for a summer, while working with Paul in the *Troy Tribune* printshop, wondering whether I should go into journalism, pursue a law career, or seek ordination. We both agreed that this decision was secondary, that the main point was to serve Christ in whatever we did and to do so by serving others. The question, of course, was how to do that best. I was led to believe that as Paul had decided to live out his faith in public service as a layman, I could best offer my distinctive witness as a pastor. It seemed to me a good combination. So off I went to Concordia Seminary.

Serving on the Lower East Side

In 1961 I became pastor of Trinity Lutheran Church, a small inner-city congregation on the Lower East Side of New York. I was immediately immersed in the lives of people who were economically very poor. Precinct Nine covered less than a square mile but contained more than a hundred thousand people. Most of them were crowded into old, five-story tenement apartments, the rest into several large, low-income public housing projects. The tenements had been built in the nineteenth century to house the waves of immigrants who had landed on Ellis Island and then started their lives as Americans on the Lower East Side. My part of the Lower East Side, around Tompkins Square Park, was a fascinating area, throbbing with life in the raw. Remnants of earlier immigrations—Germans, Irish, Italians, Jews, Ukrainians, Poles, Chinese—still lived there, often in clusters, as did the newer immigrants, mainly blacks from the South and Puerto Ricans. This fascinating, cosmopolitan mix was a great strength of the neighborhood. But in some respects Precinct Nine had the characteristics of countless other slums: high rates of poverty, crime, drug abuse, and unemployment, neighborhoods plagued by frequent fires, broken homes, and much more.

The congregation of Trinity Lutheran was composed mainly

of economically poor people, but we developed a fine sense of community, and on Sundays our celebration of the gospel was warm and exciting. The members were truly a gift of God, and they opened their hearts and lives to me. I learned more from them about the fears, hopes, and struggles of humanity than I ever dreamed possible.

It quickly became apparent that we as a congregation could not preach the gospel without also attending to some serious human problems. My favorite Peanuts cartoon, a commentary on James 2:15-17, depicts the situation eloquently. In the first frame Snoopy is shown shivering in the snow. Along comes a well-bundled Linus, who pats him on the head and says, "Be of good cheer, be warmed and clothed"—and walks away. In the last frame Snoopy is again shivering alone in the snow, but now has a big question mark over his head. We did not want to be like Linus. How could our congregation celebrate God's saving love in Christ and invite others to share it without expressing that love in response to the critical problems that plagued these people: a lost job, an empty refrigerator, no heat in the dead of winter, a crumbling marriage, a child on drugs? The people of the neighborhood had a sixth sense for con artists. They had been exploited too often, and so they approached any stranger, any offer, with skepticism. Anyone trying to reach them had to demonstrate genuine friendship, usually over a long period of time, before they were receptive to words about love.

Before long it also became apparent that dealing with problems through direct personal assistance, though essential, was not enough. Many problems were clearly rooted in larger social inequities. These needed correction through some form of public improvement—reforms in housing laws or regulations, or perhaps changes in the way those laws or regulations were being (or not being) administered. Often this meant mobilizing people in the neighborhood to act collectively to bring about change: to start job-training programs, a neighborhood clinic, housing renovation, and the like. My father used to say, "It's better to build a fence at the top of a cliff than to provide an ambulance at the bottom." So the congregation became involved in neighborhood issues, not always seeing the way clearly, but knowing that these issues had to be addressed. And we saw this involvement not as a departure from our life as a faith-centered congregation but as an expression of it.

Let me be clear. As a congregation our primary contribution to the neighborhood was nourishing people in the gospel and fostering a community of faith. This is the unique and transcendent purpose of the church. At the same time, we recognized that the living out of faith cannot be detached from other human needs, and those needs have to be addressed through public reforms as well as through direct personal service. Otherwise we deal only with symptoms and neglect causes.

Hunger was common on the Lower East Side. During the 1960s people in the neighborhood were assisted mainly through the distribution of surplus government commodities. Many of them were malnourished. A nutritional survey of 619 children in six primary schools in my neighborhood showed that the diets of three-fourths of the children were inadequate. Clinical examination showed that one out of six children was in poor health, indicated by such signs as excessive leanness and a prominent abdomen. I was unaware of the study at the time, but I did know that people frequently faced an empty refrigerator during the last week of the month and had diets that helped to fill their stomachs but did not always nourish their bodies properly. The situation improved vastly when the food-stamp program became operative. As the Lower East Side illustrated, hunger in the United States is not as pervasive and seldom as extreme as it is in most poor countries. Still, hunger is hunger, and that it was occurring in the shadow of Manhattan's skyscrapers, within walking distance of Madison Avenue in one direction and Wall Street in the other, struck me as a brutal contradiction.

Developing a Christian Citizens' Movement

One Wednesday evening during Lent in 1969, as a part of a series of topical discussions and worship services at Trinity, we talked about hunger. Ideas of how to respond to the problem abounded, including one suggestion that we write letters about hunger to our senators and representative in Congress and put the letters in the collection basket as part of our offering to God. (This approach later became an important part of Bread for the

World's strategy.) Someone suggested that we compile the ideas and send them to our national church headquarters in St. Louis for consideration at the next convention of the Lutheran Church—Missouri Synod. That left me in the position of having to read more about world hunger so that I could frame a sensible resolution incorporating these ideas. The resolution led to the establishment of a church commission to pursue the matter. In the process of preparing for action on the resolution, I felt a tug that would not go away. I began to study world hunger more seriously and arranged a leave of absence from the parish for that purpose. Several years later I was deeply immersed in helping to found Bread for the World as an interdenominational Christian citizens' movement on hunger.

I relate this story because it is important to understand that Bread for the World did not back into an artificial relationship with the church. Rather, it emerged from a ministry of the gospel and from a community of faith in which there was a shared experience of hunger and poverty. And when the organizers of Bread for the World planned the movement conceptually, our collective understanding coincided with my own experience on the Lower East Side. We felt that the churches were doing an outstanding job of directly assisting hungry people around the world through their relief and development agencies, but that almost nothing was being done to invite Christians to be responsible as *citizens* in addressing hunger—despite the fact that a single action by Congress or the president could often have a massive impact on hungry people. We were convinced that the task of Bread for the World was not to duplicate the direct assistance that the churches were already providing but to attempt to get at some of the underlying causes of hunger through better national policies.

When Bread for the World began organizing in 1974, we had two basic ideas. One was that we could help hungry people if we focused on specific decisions before Congress and the Administration. In order to achieve that goal, we began inviting Christians throughout the country to join a membership network, organized by state and congressional district, for the purpose of contacting national leaders about the problem of hunger. Our second idea was that we should engage in this work specifically and intentionally as a response to the gospel.

We believed that Christians needed to realize that just as direct assistance to poor and hungry people is a response to the gospel, so are efforts to help them by means of better public policies. Policy decisions often deal with some of the causes of hunger and poverty, and on a much larger scale than private efforts. We fully appreciated the importance of private assistance and believed that it should increase. But we saw that almost nothing was being done to challenge and mobilize U.S. Christians in America to respond to the world hunger crisis through the considerable and powerful instrument of their citizenship. With respect to the hunger issue, at least, citizenship seemed a largely wasted gift—a state of affairs hardly consistent with good stewardship.

Bread for the World's first major test began in 1975, when it launched a campaign to get Congress to pass the Right-to-Food Resolution. Our staff had drafted a resolution, and, together with Senator Mark Hatfield's staff and others on Capitol Hill, they developed a declaration of intent on hunger that Hatfield (R-Ore.) and Congressman Donald Fraser (D-Minn., now mayor of Minneapolis) were ready to sponsor. The resolution declared that because without food the right to life is denied, every person on earth should have access to a nutritionally adequate diet. The resolution was cast primarily in terms of economic development that would provide self-help opportunities to poor people.

When the resolution was introduced in Congress, it made no waves—none at all. It evoked scarcely a yawn until we organized a nationwide "Offering of Letters" to members of Congress in which hundreds of congregations across the country participated. Soon U.S. representatives and senators were receiving an impressive flow of mail in support of the resolution. It rapidly became an issue of interest in Congress and began working its way through the committee process. In instance after instance, Bread for the World members met with their representatives in Congress to discuss the issue, and frequently members of Congress were won over in this manner. For example, after Congressman Charles Grassley (R-Ia., now a U.S. senator) announced his opposition to the resolution, members and friends of Bread for the World invited him to a meeting at a church in Waverly, Iowa. They discussed the resolution at length and urged Grassley to reconsider. He did. When the *Wall Street Journal* later endorsed the measure in a lead editorial, Grassley placed the editorial in the Congressional Record and announced his support of the resolution.

Of course, a resolution is just that—a resolution. It can be a worthless piece of paper or a launching pad. The difference was illustrated in a discussion I had with Congressman Tom Foley (D-Wash.), then chairman of the House Agriculture Committee, at a time when the resolution was bottled up in committee process. Foley was personally supportive and helpful behind the scenes on this and other issues. But he had a tough committee to deal with. He told me, "Some of my committee members say, 'A right-to-food resolution is okay. But if we approve that, the next thing you know, somebody is going to come along and say that means we should have a grain reserve.' " I said nothing to Foley at the time, but in fact, legislation to establish grain reserves was precisely what we were already preparing as a follow-up to the Right-to-Food Resolution—and Foley helped us get both.

The Right-to-Food Resolution eventually passed both houses of Congress, and on the basis of this momentum we asked Congress to establish not one but two reserves: a farmer-owned grain reserve, which has helped stabilize the price and supply of grain to the benefit of farmers and consumers worldwide; and a government-owned emergency wheat reserve, which serves as insurance against famines in other parts of the world. The first reserve serves as a buffer—for example, it helps cushion sagging prices when grain production exceeds market demand. The second reserve is tapped during times of need like those in the mid-1980s, when many African countries faced famines. Each reserve was established, despite great initial resistance, because a nationwide network of citizen advocates spoke out. Each reserve has contributed to world food security. And each reserve illustrates the way in which "citizen power" can achieve benefits that are absolutely essential to millions of hungry people.

The Right-to-Food Resolution, the two grain reserves, and various other initiatives that Bread for the World has successfully launched do not mean that we are now on the way toward ending hunger. Although the United States has taken some important steps toward that end, we have also taken some backward steps, and the footwork tends to be haphazard—here a little, there a little. As a nation we have not yet made the elimination of hunger a major foreign-policy objective. We have tinkered with solutions, but we have not made finding them a top priority. Nevertheless, citizen action in this area has helped to alert Congress, inform the public, obtain policy actions of far-reaching significance for hungry people, and make a future national commitment against world hunger at least more plausible.

Recognizing the Need for Citizen Advocates

Let me illustrate in a different way the importance of citizen advocacy.

In 1968 the late Barbara Ward, a devout British Christian and internationally respected development economist, attended a worldwide conference of church leaders and lay professionals, the purpose of which was to examine the church's role in a world of hunger and poverty. As often happens at church conferences, impressive resolutions were drafted. Barbara Ward was excited. After the conference she came to this country and told an informal gathering of U.S. senators and representatives that the churches in the United States and around the world were about to build broad public support for a major global effort against hunger and poverty.

Silence filled the room.

"I'll call you when I get the first letter," responded the junior senator from Minnesota.

A few years later, about the time that Bread for the World was getting started, I heard Walter Mondale tell that story. Then he added, "I haven't had to make that call yet."

Why not?

Where are the Christians? Where are the people who care?

I'm convinced that there are many who care and care deeply. You will find them in our churches every Sunday. Of course, there is plenty of apathy—each of us can attest to that within ourselves. But there is also a great deal of compassion. Christians do care when others suffer, and we are often willing to make personal sacrifices to help if we know that a particular action will make an important difference. One way that we show our concern is by contributing to hunger appeals. But we have not learned to express our concern about hunger to those who make national policy decisions. Perhaps this is so because we are unsure what policies could provide solutions to the problem of hunger. The result, in any case, is that government leaders have not heard from us, or have not heard from us in a way that is effective, and consequently they have made the issue of hunger a relatively low priority.

What I say about hunger could be applied to a host of issues related to social justice and the well-being of others. It applies with particular force to hunger because few of the world's hungry can speak for themselves to U.S. decision-makers. Most are powerless in the halls of Congress and in the Administration unless others speak on their behalf. That's our responsibility—and our great opportunity. Unless we call attention to their suffering and specify action that is needed, we can be sure that they will be largely disregarded when national decisions are made. And when these people are overlooked, initiatives that could provide hope and opportunity for people throughout the world will not be taken; instead, measures that (perhaps unwittingly) make them permanent victims of hunger will be enacted. It happens all the time.

It is not that our leaders are especially callous or cruel. But they are not apt to know or have time to think much about policy choices that may affect the lives of impoverished people on other continents. After all, they are daily overwhelmed by many complex issues that have vocal constituencies. Because they want to be re-elected, they are well-attuned to those constituencies, to the opinions and pressures of the voters back home. Most members of Congress would probably like to be on the side of the angels, but angels do not vote, and they do not present their case—at least not directly—to Congress. So if members of Congress must choose between the angels and the voters, the voters will probably get preferential treatment.

I remember my brother Paul's disappointment during his first term in the Illinois state assembly when he discovered what issues most aroused the people in his district. For example, dozens of letters came in advising him on legislation relating to the length of the duck-hunting season, but only two letters commented on major action that had to be taken regarding the deplorable situation of mentally retarded persons living in state institutions. You can guess which issue received more attention.

My point is not that duck hunters should quit offering advice, but that Christians—at least a *few* Christians—ought to care enough about decent treatment for the mentally retarded to write state legislators on their behalf.

Therein lies a dilemma, but also an opportunity. The opportunity is that of developing public support for measures that safeguard the mentally retarded or provide hungry people with a chance to work their way out of hunger and poverty. The opportunity is to reach decision-makers on key issues, to make them feel that if they vote with the angels, they will also enjoy the support of some voters.

In saying this I am clearly inviting Christians to involve themselves in the political arena. Isn't such involvement a risky mixture of religion and politics, perhaps one that is even at odds with the gospel?

No, it is not.

Let me suggest a fundamental distinction, one that undergirds my thinking: the distinction between the separation of church and state on the one hand, and the separation of religion and life on the other hand. The separation of church and state, properly understood, is a principle of fundamental importance to the nation. The separation of religion from life is pure heresy. It is false because it contradicts the biblical witness and therefore the Christian understanding of faith. To take major areas of life, those having to do with social and economic decisions that vitally affect all of us, and put them into a compartment carefully separated from faith is to turn much of life over to the devil. It is another way of making Christianity into a one-hour-on-Sunday religion, or perhaps a faith that has to do with one's personal moral values but not, say, with one's business or professional career and certainly not—God forbid!—with politics. This view is heresy because it locks God out of much of life. It is the opposite of confessing Jesus as Lord.

Of course, we do not live in a risk-free world. I will have more to say about the importance of using careful judgment in relating religion to politics. My appeal is not for the church as church to become involved in partisan politics, but for Christians as citizens to use their influence to help shape public policies that can, among other things, insure life and opportunity for many who would otherwise face needless suffering.

I know there is resistance to such an appeal. But I believe that Christians will increasingly respond to it provided they recognize

- that policy change is essential if we are to respond effectively to human need.
- that efforts to change public policy are not alien to the gospel but can be an authentic expression of our life in Christ.

I want to make the case for citizen action and show how we can choose policies that move us toward goals that are dear to the heart of God.

Chapter 2

The Biblical Roots of Social Concern

> The interest of Jesus extended to the ones who wept for the harsh realities of life: the sick and the lame crawling out of the huts which lay squeezed together beyond the poverty-stricken town and hamlets.
>
> His heart ached at the sight. Love and sympathy flowed from him like blood from a deep wound. We in our hearts know how we are attracted to glamorous and beautiful people and how we easily close our eyes to those who are filthy and ugly. It was different with Jesus, whose predilection was for the lepers and the harlots whom others despised.
>
> —Shusaku Endo, *A Life of Jesus*

> To try to improve society is not worldliness but love. To wash your hands of society is not love but worldliness.
>
> —Sir Frederick Catherwood

> Jesus came to liberate us from sin, but for something, as well. We miss half the good news. The good news is always better than we thought it was.
>
> —John Walsh, M.M.

I was on the phone with Stan Mooneyham, former president of World Vision International, to tell him that the nominations committee of Bread for the World's board of directors wanted him to run for a position on the board. Would he consider it?

Stan began asking a number of probing questions to make sure that, if he ran and was elected, we would be a good match for each other.

"What's the most radical piece you've ever published?" he asked.

"*Cry Justice*," I replied without hesitation. (*Cry Justice* by Ron Sider is a collection of excerpts from the Bible about hunger and poverty.)

Stan regarded Bread for the World highly, but I knew why he was asking the question. He wanted to make sure we had no unadvertised ideological bias that would make it uncomfortable for him to serve on our board. Stan laughed with delight at my answer because he knew that the Bible contains a profound call to discipleship regarding hunger and poverty. *Cry Justice* is only a sampling of the biblical treasure on this subject, but it is a powerful little book. One can hardly read it without feeling something of the overwhelming concern that God has for the poor and the hungry, without realizing that God calls us to a special accountability regarding their suffering. God's concern is neither marginal nor shallow. It is central and deep. It is reflected in the law, in the prophets, and in the wisdom literature. It is embedded in that old hymnbook of the Hebrews, the Psalms. And it is featured in the witness of the apostles and of Jesus himself. It is an awesome testimony, and the wonder is that so many of us could escape noticing it. But perhaps this too is a case of what Jesus meant when he said, "This people will listen and listen, but not understand; they will look and look, but not see" (Matt. 13:14; cf. Isa. 6:9, TEV).

The Hebrew Scriptures and the Oppressed

In both the Old and the New Testament, the crucial starting point in considering God's concern for the poor is a central act of liberation, an act with which any examination of biblical ethics must begin. In the Old Testament the Exodus stands out as a special action of God that more than any other revealed to the Israelites who God was. This event illuminated the nature of God and God's plan for the nation—indeed, for the world—as no other event did prior to the coming of Jesus. The Exodus told the Hebrew people not only who God is but also who they were. The central place of this event is celebrated in the Passover, the pre-eminent religious festival of the Jews. All Old Testament theology flows from and relates to this dramatic intervention of God in history to rescue his chosen people from slavery. I say "chosen people," and rightly so—but this phrase is misleading because it has a noble ring to it, much as the cross, a means of execution, has become a decoration piece that lulls when it should startle. In the same way, the designation "chosen people" tends to obscure the fact that God reached out to rescue people at the very bottom of the social and economic heap, the "nobodies" who were trampled on, exploited, abused, despised, and rejected. In the words of a flippant and perhaps derisive rhyme, "How odd of God / To choose the Jews." Odd? No, but unpredictable and contrary to all human expectation. That is the way God encounters the human race. The same sort of surprise, the same disregard for the world's carefully constructed order of importance, later characterized the coming of God in Jesus of Nazareth.

So we start with the Exodus, acknowledging that near the center of what God wants us to understand about himself, ourselves, and others is that he chose to show an extraordinary love to a group of oppressed slaves. He liberated them and made a special covenant with them, promising to be their God and accept them as his people.

To be chosen is not only to be loved but also to be challenged to respond with love. Thus the Exodus provides our point of departure for understanding the purpose and responsibility of God's people. The Ten Commandments illustrate the fundamental importance of this event in a way we often overlook. Many of us memorized the commandments when we were young. We started with the first one: "Thou shalt have no other gods before me." But in doing so we had already missed the statement that introduces all of the commandments and provides the context for their understanding. Exodus 20 begins this way: "God spoke, and these were his words: 'I am the Lord your God who brought you out of of Egypt, where you were slaves' " (vv. 1-2, TEV). And then come the commandments. An unwritten but eloquent "therefore" rings out to connect each of the commandments to God's rescue of his people from slavery: "I brought you out of bondage, and therefore you shall have no other gods, therefore you shall remember the Sabbath," and so on.

Respect for human life grows out of gratitude to God for freeing the Hebrew people when they were oppressed and establishing a covenant with them. God's love for the oppressed, so evident in the Exodus, becomes pivotal in the way we relate to others. There are no categories of people so low or so distant that respect for them is unnecessary, that personal obligations and legal protections do not apply to them; we cannot make the circle of responsibility—in effect, the circle of humanity—small. That's what the lawyer was trying to do when he asked Jesus, "Who *is* my neighbor?" As if to say, "Tell me who my neighbors are so I can love them and be free of obligation to others." Jesus replied by telling the story of the despised Samaritan who helped a brutally assaulted Jew (see Luke 10:29-37). And then Jesus turned the question around by asking the lawyer, "Who *acted as neighbor* to the stricken man?" Here Jesus faithfully reflected the God of the Exodus, whose rescue of slaves informs our understanding of God's law.

We find that the Exodus experience shaped not only the Ten Commandments but also the more detailed codes that were to guide the conduct of the Israelites. Over and over again the instruction to remember the foreigner, the widow, and the orphan—those most vulnerable to hunger and poverty—is tied to the Exodus. Take, for example, the instruction found in Deuteronomy 24:17-19, 21-23 (TEV):

> Do not deprive foreigners and orphans of their rights; and do not take a widow's garment as security for a loan. Remember that you were slaves in Egypt and that the Lord your God set you free; that is why I have given you this command.
>
> When you gather your crops and fail to bring in some of the grain that you have cut, do not go back for it; it is to be left for the foreigners, orphans, and widows. . . . When you have gathered your grapes once, do not go back over the vines a second time; the grapes that are left are for the foreigners, orphans, and widows. Never forget that you were slaves in Egypt; that is why I have given you this command.

Other laws provided for sharing part of a tithe (one-tenth) of the harvest with foreigners, orphans, and widows (Deut. 14:28-29), for lending at no interest to those in need (Exod. 22:25), and for the cancellation of debts every seventh year (Deut. 15:1-2, 7-11). In addition, every fiftieth year was designated the Year of Jubilee, during which time property that had been bought was to be returned to the family of the original owner (Lv. 25:8-28). Although there is no record in the Old Testament that this restoration of land was carried out, the intention behind the

instruction was clear: to prevent the concentration of wealth and
to preserve a relatively equal distribution of land while under-
scoring the fact that the land in reality belonged to the Lord.

Closely linked to the Exodus and its impact on the laws that
governed the life of the people is the theme of *justice* in the Old
Testament. One instruction concerning justice required everyone to be judged on the same basis. Judges were to be impartial
and fair in making decisions. Judges and other officials were not
to receive gifts, "for gifts blind the eyes even of wise and honest
men, and cause them to give wrong decisions" (Deut. 16:19,
TEV). This instruction was especially important to insure that
the poor—the usual victims of partiality—would not be treated
unfairly (Exod. 23:6). Justice in this sense is well depicted by
the figure in U.S. courthouses: a blindfolded woman holding a
balance scale.

But for the Hebrews the idea of justice went far beyond the
notion of impartiality, just as the Hebrew idea of peace *(shalom)*
meant more than the absence of war. Justice embraced a sense
of fairness and wholeness in relationships; the goal was that
families and communities and finally the entire nation experience well-being. The Exodus shaped the Hebrew sense of justice,
which included the aim that no one among them be poor. Consequently, the prophets excoriated people who took advantage
of the poor. Amos, for example, denounced those who trampled
on the needy and destroyed the poor in order to gain wealth
(2:6-7; 8:4-6). And he railed against the men and women of Israel
who reveled in luxury while the poor were crushed (4:1; 6:1-7).
Isaiah was no less severe in his pronouncements:

> The Lord is ready to state his case; he is ready to judge his people.
> The Lord is bringing the elders and leaders of his people to judg-
> ment. He makes this accusation: "You have plundered vineyards,
> and your houses are full of what you have taken from the poor. You
> have no right to crush my people and take advantage of the poor. I,
> the Sovereign Lord Almighty, have spoken." (3:13-15, TEV)

In short, the prophets were far from delicate in denouncing injustice. The judgment they announced included punishments
such as violence, captivity, and loss of life and family.

The prophets also rejected worship that was detached from
justice. According to Amos, "The Lord says, 'I hate your reli-

gious festivals. . . . Stop your noisy songs. . . . Instead, let justice flow like a stream, and righteousness like a river that never goes dry' " (5:21, 23-24, TEV).

The same religion-and-life theme occurs elsewhere in the writings of the prophets, who combined warnings with the promise given in these lines of Isaiah 58:

> The kind of fasting I want is this: Remove the chains of oppression and the yoke of injustice, and let the oppressed go free. Share your food with the hungry and open your homes to the homeless poor. Give clothes to those who have nothing to wear, and do not refuse to help your own relatives.
>
> Then my favor will shine on you like the morning sun, and your wounds will be quickly healed. I will always be with you to save you; my presence will protect you on every side. When you pray, I will answer you. When you call to me, I will respond.
>
> If you put an end to oppression, to every gesture of contempt, and to every evil word; if you give food to the hungry and satisfy those who are in need, then the darkness around you will turn to the brightness of noon. (Vv. 6-10, TEV)

The Psalms invite us again and again to sing of God's passion for justice. Psalm 41 declares, "Happy are those who are concerned for the poor; / the Lord will help them when they are in trouble" (v. 1, TEV). Psalm 72 makes the following plea:

> Teach the king to judge with your righteousness, O God;
> > share with him your own justice,
> so that he will rule over your people with justice
> > and govern the oppressed with righteousness. . . .
> May the king judge the poor fairly;
> > may he help the needy
> > and defeat their oppressors. (Vv. 1-2, 4, TEV)

And Psalm 146 offers this description of God's justice:

> He always keeps his promises;
> > he judges in favor of the oppressed
> > and gives food to the hungry.
> The Lord sets prisoners free
> > and gives sight to the blind.
> He lifts those who have fallen;
> > he loves his righteous people.
> He protects the strangers who live in our land;
> > he helps widows and orphans,
> > but ruins the plans of the wicked. (Vv. 6-9, TEV)

Wisdom literature also emphasizes this theme. The some-times-disillusioned writer of Ecclesiastes observes, "Then I looked again at all the injustice that goes on in this world. The oppressed were crying, and no one would help them. No one would help them, because their oppressors had power on their side" (4:1, TEV). The theme of justice appears also in Proverbs:

> If you refuse to listen to the cry of the poor, your own cry for help will not be heard. (21:13, TEV)

> A good person knows the rights of the poor, but wicked people cannot understand such things. (29:7, TEV)

> Speak up for people who cannot speak for themselves. . . . Protect the rights of the poor and needy. (31:8-9, TEV)

My point in all of this is to show that concern for the most vulnerable members of society is pervasive in the Old Testament, and that it flows directly from the revelation of God as the God who rescued an enslaved people and made them his own.

The New Testament and the Oppressed

Just as the Exodus was the pivotal point for all Old Testament thinking, so Jesus Christ became pivotal for all New Testament thought. He did so, however, in continuity with and in fulfillment of the Old Testament. As the Exodus was central to God's covenant with the Hebrews, so Jesus established a new covenant as the Lamb of God who takes away the sin of the world. Jesus' ministry, including his special esteem for the poor, showed how thoroughly his life's work emerged from his roots in the Old Testament. When Mary was pregnant with Jesus, she sang in her great Magnificat,

> He has shown strength with his arm,
> he has scattered the proud in the imagination of their hearts,
> he has put down the mighty from their thrones,
> and exalted those of low degree;
> he has filled the hungry with good things,
> and the rich he has sent empty away. (Luke 1:51-53, RSV)

The birth of Jesus, while revealing God's disposition toward the entire human family, gave special honor to those of ordinary and humble means. How odd of God to choose parents who

could find nothing better than a livestock shelter as a place for
Jesus to be born!

After his baptism, Jesus returned to his hometown of Nazareth. There he stood up in the synagogue and read from Isaiah
a passage that he clearly understood to describe himself and his
forthcoming ministry:

> The Spirit of the Lord is upon me,
> because he has anointed me to preach good news to the poor.
> He has sent me to proclaim release to the captives
> and recovering of sight to the blind,
> to set at liberty those who are oppressed,
> to proclaim the acceptable year of the Lord. (Luke 4:18-19, RSV)

The rest of Jesus' life is an unfolding of precisely such a ministry—to the offense of those who looked for a different kind of
Messiah. Even John the Baptizer had his moments. Languishing
in prison and soon to be executed, John wondered whether he
had not made a mistake in declaring Jesus to be God's anointed
one. Even John did not think Jesus appeared very messianic. He
was preaching to motley crowds, healing sick people—and letting John rot in jail. So John sent his disciples to ask Jesus
whether he was really the Promised One, or should they be
looking for someone else? Jesus' reply to John cited as evidence
those very things that made John doubt: "Go and tell John what
you have seen and heard: the blind receive their sight, the lame
walk, lepers are cleansed, and the deaf hear, the dead are raised
up, the poor have good news preached to them." Then he added,
"And blessed is he who takes no offense at me" (Luke 7:22-23,
RSV).

All four Gospels, but especially Luke, depict Jesus constantly
reaching out to those on the bottom of the social pyramid—the
poor, women, Samaritans, lepers, children, prostitutes, tax col-
lectors, and other publicly ostracized sinners—to the dismay of
those who guarded social values. Of course, Jesus was also eager
to accept people who were well-placed socially, financially, and
religiously. But he made it clear that they no less than others
needed to repent, and repent of sins that were deeply imbedded
in accomplishments for which they were publicly admired. There
was, for example, the rich young lawyer; Jesus invited him to
sell all of his possessions, give the proceeds to the poor, and

follow him. And there were the religious leaders who enjoyed
being praised for their devotion to God and God's law but who
were devoid of justice and mercy. They felt threatened by Jesus,
so his relationship with them tended to be less comfortable,
more apt to precipitate conflict.

And so it goes throughout the entire ministry of Jesus up to
and including his dramatic portrayal of the great judgment scene
in Matthew 25. He will gather all the nations before him, separating them into two groups: those who fed him when he was
hungry, clothed him when he was naked, and visited him in
prison, and those who failed to do so. The judgment he will
pronounce will surprise each group. "Lord, when did we ever
do that?" And Christ's answer will be, "When you did it—or
failed to do it—to the least of my brothers" (my paraphrase). In
the view of many New Testament scholars, the original meaning
of "the least of my brothers" is limited to followers of Jesus.
Even so, as the parable of the despised Samaritan suggests, it
can have a wider application. In any case, it says something
awesome about our accountability regarding the poor and
oppressed.

But Jesus' ministry cannot be understood apart from his death
and resurrection. As he put it, "The Son of man came not to be
served but to serve, and to give his life as a ransom for many"
(Matt. 20:28, RSV). Not only does the sacrificial death of Jesus
reveal the depth of God's love for us, but through it God takes
our place, atones for our sin, and reconciles us to himself. So
Jesus is God's extraordinary gift of grace, his undeserved, forgiving love through whom we are restored as sons and daugh-
ters to God's family.

This has immediate ethical implications. We are to "be *imi-
tators* of God, as beloved children. And walk in love, as Christ
loved us and gave himself up for us, a fragrant offering and
sacrifice to God" (Eph. 5:1-2, RSV; my italics). Clearly we are to
model our lives after that of Jesus, to embrace such fundamentals
as his concern for the poor and oppressed. That is our calling.
We are to be neighbors to those in need. And we are to do so
because of God's great love for us.

In the Lutheran tradition in which I grew up, "faith alone"
was a watchword, sometimes a slogan. We heard less than we
needed to about another part of that tradition—namely, that

although we live before God by faith alone, faith is never alone. As fire burns, so faith is active in love. One of the passages we memorized almost before we could walk was Ephesians 2:8-9: "For by grace you have been saved through faith; and this is not your own doing, it is the gift of God—not because of works, lest any man should boast" (RSV). It is a powerful summary statement of grace. But it wasn't until years later, when I was in seminary and had read Ephesians many times, that I realized that an organic part of verses 8-9 follows in verse 10: "For we are his workmanship, *created in Christ Jesus for good works,* which God prepared beforehand, that we should walk in them" (RSV, my italics). We are not saved by good works, but a life of good works flows from God's grace in Christ. In this way— through us!—God means to touch the lives of others.

The Resurrection, as part of Christ's redemptive work, liberates us from sin and death and empowers us to carry out the work of God with a courage that stems from this ultimate victory. That courage was not so much defined as it was enacted in the lives of the disciples after Pentecost. It enabled them to defy suffering and even death for their Lord. Paul linked the Resurrection with Christian action in 1 Corinthians 15. After concluding his treatise on the Resurrection with a ringing declaration of victory, Paul added: "*Therefore,* my beloved brethren, be steadfast, immovable, always abounding in the work of the Lord, knowing that in the Lord your labor is not in vain" (v. 58, RSV; my italics). The specific work immediately urged was that of helping poverty-stricken Jewish Christians.

Running through both Old and New Testaments, then, is a clear expectation regarding our relationship to others, an expectation rooted in God's redeeming love. We are called to embrace our family, our fellow believers, our community and nation, and especially those who are most vulnerable with the love and the justice that come from God.

Is God on the Side of the Poor?

Occasionally the Bible's strong identification with the poor has been summarized—incorrectly, in my view—in the words, "God is on the side of the poor." This declaration overstates the case in an effort to capture a sense of God's deep concern. If God is truly on the side of the poor, the best thing we could do for them would be to keep them poor. Surely our aspiration is not to bring them into a situation where God is no longer on their side. Of course, one may argue that God can be on other sides as well—but if God is on other sides too, then nothing is accomplished by saying that he is on the side of the poor.

Some might argue that the law against partiality is evidence of God's siding with the poor, but the law against partiality applied to rich and poor alike (see Exod. 23:3-6). True, it was primarily a defense for the poor, who were most apt to be treated unfairly in court and the most likely victims of bribes, but the law required evenhanded treatment. It rejected favoring the poor as well as the rich. Justice in this sense is blind and considers all to be equals.

Furthermore, the assertion "God is on the side of the poor" appears to make the poor a new religious elite, one based on economic deprivation, with poverty a means of grace. I find no evidence for that in the biblical writings. To be sure, the fact that God identified with Hebrew slaves and set them free makes a powerful statement about his attitude toward oppressed people—and oppressors. But there were many other slaves and many other oppressed people who did not receive this favored treatment. God's covenant with Israel was a historic development that should be respected for its uniqueness as well as for its wider applications. To suggest that the covenant relationship automatically embraces all who are poor or any and every oppressed people invites enormous confusion and makes it more difficult—not less difficult—to draw out the real and warranted implications about God's concern for the poor.

"The Lord judges in favor of the oppressed," says Psalm 103 (TEV), and I suspect that is usually the intended meaning behind "God is on the side of the poor." The difference between the two assertions may seem slight, but it is not. Psalm 103 means that if some people are being oppressed and others are oppressing them, the Lord judges in favor of the former. This declaration speaks clearly enough concerning justice and our role as citizens.

Poor people have God's special concern—and deserve ours—not because they are better people but simply because they are in distress. Those of us who are parents have an almost instinctive understanding of this. We love all of our children. But if one child gets sick, becomes physically or emotionally injured, or experiences some other great hurt, our hearts go out to that child. We pay special attention to him or her not because we love our other children less, but because this child has special need.

"The Poor You Have Always with You"

Jesus once said, "The poor you have always with you" (Mark 14:7 as frequently translated and used). Few sayings of Jesus have been misused so often. Those who quote it frequently imply that we are stuck with the poor and will always be plagued by poverty, so there's no use trying to do much about it. But this interpretation is wrong on several counts:

1. It is abundantly clear elsewhere in the Bible that this is neither the position of Jesus nor that of any of the biblical writers.

2. Jesus made the statement in a very particular situation: when Mary of Bethany was anointing his feet in a burial ritual on the eve of his crucifixion. Jesus was saying that the moment and the occasion were unique. The world's savior was about to be killed, and one repentant sinner, who sensed what lay ahead better than the disciples did, was making a profound gesture of love. Don't prevent her from doing this beautiful thing, he told them.

3. The disciples objected that the ointment could have been sold and the proceeds given to the poor. Their protest indicates that Jesus had taught them well. The needs of the poor were indeed a foremost concern of his followers.

4. Jesus told his followers, "You will always have the poor with you, and you will never fail for opportunities to help them, but you will not have me with you much longer" (Mark 14:7, my paraphrase). Far from discouraging assistance to the poor, he was encouraging it, as he always had. Jesus' statement about the poor was drawn from Deuteronomy 15:11, which adds, "therefore I command you, You shall open wide your hand to your brother, to the needy and to the poor, in the land" (RSV). This command is part of a section of the law regarding the sharing of the tithe of the harvest with sojourners, orphans, and widows, and the forgiveness of all debts every seven years, with

the explicit goal that "there will be no poor among you" (Deut. 15:4, RSV).

In short, a closer examination of this saying of Jesus strongly supports his concern for the poor and does not lift our responsibility in that regard.

Are Poverty and Riches Just Rewards?

The link between poverty and laziness disturbs many people. Are people poor because they are lazy? Are riches a reward for hard work and a sign of God's blessing? The answer to both questions is a qualified "No." To be sure, the biblical tradition does encourage diligence and hard work. "Go to the ant, thou sluggard," says a proverb (Prov. 6:6, KJV). And Saint Paul said, "If any one will not work, let him not eat" (2 Thess. 3:10, RSV).[1] Unfortunately, Paul's statement is often twisted to mean that if people are not eating, they must be unwilling to work.

No one can deny that some people are poor because they are lazy. But most poor people who are able to work are willing and eager to do so. During World War II, when there were jobs for everyone, there was virtually no unemployment in the United States. For twenty-one years I lived in a poverty-stricken neighborhood in New York. The vast majority of unemployed persons wanted to work. Some were handicapped by limited skills, poor education, or emotional or physical disorders. Others were on drugs or engaged in criminal behavior. In some cases the welfare syndrome and the cycle of poverty carried over from one generation to another and clearly discouraged a work ethic. However, given the opportunity, most unemployed poor people would gladly work to improve their circumstances. The vast majority of employable poor people, it should be remembered, *are* employed.

1. The background to Paul's statement is revealing. In one of the letters he wrote to the church in Thessalonica, Paul stressed that the Lord would be coming soon. Some who heard that interpreted "soon" to mean "very soon indeed" and concluded that the best thing to do would be to sit and wait. What was the point of working to improve the order of things if it would soon be superseded by the kingdom of God? If the kingdom is everything and the affairs of this world are nothing, why exert oneself for the latter? This viewpoint misses the connection between life in Christ and life in the world—and it is a viewpoint that Paul rejected.

What is seen as laziness sometimes turns out to be lack of energy due to malnutrition or ill health. Moritz Thomsen, a farmer from the state of Washington who was one of the earliest Peace Corps volunteers, wrote of his experience in rural Ecuador. Thomsen was outraged by the "laziness" of the villagers until circumstances forced him to eat what they ate. He quickly learned why many of the world's farmers are able to work only three or four hours a day. "There are just so many miles to a gallon of bananas," he observed.[2]

During the 1980s famine in northern Mozambique, I saw a planeload of corn being unloaded in an area that was not accessible by truck. I was told that when the shipments first came in, those unloading did their work so slowly that it delayed the distribution of the supplies. Then the relief workers learned that those unloading the corn were living on the same food ration that other recipients received—an amount that fell below the minimum daily requirement for sustenance. So the workers were given an additional ration of corn, enough for an extra meal each day. That extra meal translated immediately into energy and fast work that put the shipments back on schedule.

The view that the poor are lazy makes a blanket moral judgment against them. I suspect that poverty stems from laziness much less often than prosperity stems from greed. Ironically, we do not label everyone who succeeds as greedy, but we do tend to blame the poor for their economic condition and see poverty as a sign of moral failure. How different is the attitude conveyed in the Bible, where the poor are frequently seen as victims of oppression, and always respected as human beings eminently worthy of God's—and our—special concern.

What about the view that riches are a sign of God's favor? The biblical record is mixed. Prosperity is sometimes so regarded—though this view is usually expressed in such a way that it applies to an entire people, not individuals. Further, prosperity means sufficiency rather than excess. It denotes well-being and fullness of life, not merely material abundance. As we have seen, the prophets often denounced the rich for accumulating wealth while others went hungry. And the Psalmist frequently

2. Thomsen, *Living Poor: A Peace Corps Chronicle* (Seattle: University of Washington Press, 1969), p. 84.

asked, "Why do the wicked prosper and the righteous suffer?" It is dangerous—indeed, heretical—to look upon one's own prosperity as a sign of moral superiority. If prosperity has been achieved honorably, it may be seen as a blessing from God. But, as with all blessings, God is the giver, and he entrusts any measure of wealth to an individual with the express intention that it be used not self-indulgently and at the expense of others but in a way that furthers justice and brings opportunity to others. Anything less than this invites the judgment of God, for "to whom much is given, of him will much be required" (Luke 12:48, RSV). This is not language designed to countenance greed or pride. "But woe to you that are rich, for you have received your consolation," Jesus said (Luke 6:24, RSV). He also observed that "it is easier for a camel to go through the eye of a needle than for a rich man to enter the kingdom of God" (Mark 10:25, RSV). In few aspects of life are we so prone to idolatry and self-deception as in matters concerning our own material advantage.

Public Policy and Citizenship

The Bible prescribes no economic policy, foreign policy, or government structures for us, nor does it detail for us the way in which we are to carry out our responsibilities as U.S. citizens in the twentieth century. The Bible gives us a sense of direction, but it leaves the method of traveling to us.

Biblical Israel was a tiny, rural, and small-town nation whose experience antedated ours by several thousand years. As a covenant people, its experience was unique. Although Israel went through various stages and forms of government, it was in principle a theocracy, a nation ruled by God. The lines between religious and civil laws were not clearly drawn. For these and other reasons, we cannot impose Old Testament patterns on modern industrial states. Gleaning and tithing from harvests, for example, would not provide solutions to hunger in our country, although they may offer us some clues.

Regarding our responsibilities as citizens, the Bible speaks with authority about values but offers no step-by-step guidelines. As citizens of a theocracy, the Israelites participated simultaneously and inescapably in civil and religious life. That doesn't offer much of a model for a democracy such as ours, with its separation of church and state. New Testament comments on citizenship are quite limited partly because so few Christians in the Roman Empire possessed full citizenship. So they were encouraged to "pray, pay, and obey"—pray for those in authority, pay their taxes, and obey the law. The apostle Paul was an exception. He was a Roman citizen by virtue of his birth in Tarsus, and he didn't hesitate to invoke his citizenship when he needed to avoid floggings, get out of jail, or appeal for a fair trial. Even at that, Paul's opportunities for exercising citizenship were limited compared to our own. In addition, for the first few decades of the church's existence, believers were a tiny minority of the population, and they anticipated the early return of Jesus. For these reasons, they had little opportunity and saw no need to construct a social ethics for responsible citizenship.

Conclusion

From the witness of the Old and New Testaments emerges a strong sense of moral obligation to the poor and oppressed, a "bias" that is rooted first in God's work of rescuing an enslaved people and establishing a covenant with them, and ultimately in God's redemptive love in Jesus Christ. God's action and biblical testimony are of monumental importance in the shaping of our desires and actions as Christians. However, they take us only part of the way on our journey to seek justice in today's world. The Bible offers us no Christian economic system, no political blueprint, no proof texts for domestic or foreign policy. But it does give us a solid foundation on which to build.

Chapter 3
Public Intervention or Private Aid?

Philanthropy combines genuine pity with the display of power
... [but] the powerful are more inclined to be generous than
to grant social justice.

—Reinhold Niebuhr, *Moral Man and Immoral Society*

[The Gospel] summons people to repent of social as well as
personal sins.

—Lausanne Occasional Papers

I brought food to the hungry, and people called me a saint;
I asked why people were hungry, and people called me a
communist.

—Bishop Dom Helder Camara

In October 1984 I was a guest on the Jami McFerran Show, a call-in program of station KCMO in Kansas City. I discussed the African famine and the need for a more vigorous U.S. response. Over one of the phone lines came an agitated voice. "What you're doing is very un-Christian!" the caller said. "You're forcing people to contribute their taxes to what you think is a good idea. You want to redistribute wealth by force. I say by the Word of God that you are wrong!"

The Role of Government

The caller expressed a discomfort with the role of government that many others share. A strong biblical case for Christian engagement in the fight against hunger and poverty does not self-evidently lead to the conclusion that we should call upon the government to take action. Isn't that asking the government to do what we should be doing voluntarily? And are we not, therefore, abdicating our responsibility as Christians and as the church by trying to get the government to do what we are unwilling to do?

These questions may stem from opposition in principle to government intervention of almost any kind except in matters of national defense and public safety. But such opposition does not spring from divine revelation, which views government as a means designed by God for restraining evil and promoting justice. Those in authority are described by the apostle Paul as "God's servant[s] for your good" (Rom. 13:4, RSV). Although Paul focused on obedience because he was writing to Christians who were subject to a government in which they had no voice, it is fair to assume that he would have said much more to Christians living in a democracy. Paul's teaching that governmental authority comes from God and that those in authority are to use it for the good of those governed contradicted the official wisdom of the Roman Empire, as Bernard Zylstra has pointed out: "Political absolutism, ancient or modern, proceeds from the notion that the citizen exists for the good of the state. Paul argues the exact opposite: the state and its authorities exist for the good of the citizenry. . . . That good is public justice."[1]

An illustration of the government's role—and our responsibility in determining that role—crossed my desk recently in the form of a printed letter from Robert V. Schnabel, president of Valparaiso University. Schnabel reported that President Reagan's budget proposals for 1987-88 would eliminate at least $500,000 in government-sponsored loans to Valparaiso students, placing their future at that university in jeopardy. He asked that letters be sent to U.S. senators and representatives about this matter. Then he added that the purpose of the federal government involves more than providing for the common defense. "[It] also includes promoting the general welfare and securing the blessings of liberty for us and our posterity. The general welfare and the blessings of liberty require an educated populace."

1. Zylstra, "The Bible, Justice and the State," in *Confessing Christ and Doing Politics*, ed. James W. Skillen (Washington: Association for Public Justice Education Fund, 1982), p. 46.

Though it says much about nongovernmental activity, the Bible does not describe for us the most appropriate role for government regarding higher education, the African famine, or most other issues. But it does tell us that governments have a positive obligation to promote justice. Because ours is a government of the people, not above the people, and because we choose our leaders and have a voice in determining government policies, our responsibility for what our government does or fails to do is considerable.

Christians will not always arrive at the same conclusions regarding the proper role of government in responding to specific social problems, but they can consider the matter within a common biblical framework. This is a trail that I cannot further explore here. But let me say in passing that I believe that the government should, first of all, encourage nongovernmental responses—responses that will, for example, strengthen the family and enable the private sector to create jobs. The government can often be a catalyst for or simply provide freedom for nongovernmental solutions, and it should not try to displace nongovernmental institutions and efforts. But because it has a responsibility to promote public justice, the government often needs to do (or assure the doing of) what cannot or will not be done adequately without its initiative.

In this country the case for reducing the role of government to matters of national defense and public safety has already been widely rejected. The government builds roads, schools, hospitals, and water and sewage facilities, provides social security, regulates interstate commerce, protects civil rights, and does a great many other things for the common good. Through our elected officials we make many decisions that affect the entire nation. The making of such decisions and the collection of taxes to carry them out is the way our republican form of government works. The process is democratic. It provides some assurance that the will of the majority is being carried out. We can participate in this process by speaking up for policies that we believe to be beneficial—such as, in my opinion, assistance for victims of the African famine—and against policies we oppose. We can also work and vote to elect officials who will represent our point of view on issues that are important to us. Regarding hunger and poverty, the argument today is not so much *whether* the

government should address these issues but *how* it can do so
most effectively. For example, the ongoing public debate is not
about whether we should have an economic "safety net" for
people, but how the safety net should be constructed and who
should benefit from it under what circumstances.

Examining Motives

Discomfort with government attempts to alleviate hunger and
poverty seldom stems from complete opposition to public intervention. Sometimes it reflects a view that government action
needs to be restricted so that it does not impede individual freedom. More often, practical and personal considerations probably
come into play. Some of these are legitimate—say, the desire
that government efforts be cost-effective, and the fear that they
are not. But our views are often primarily motivated (and always
at least partly motivated) by impulses that do not flatter us—the
love of money, for example. If I am upset because governmental
action means higher taxes for me, I should ask whether my primary motive is a desire to help others or old-fashioned greed.

Another consideration sometimes associated with greed is
hostility toward victims of poverty. This attitude may be expressed quite openly ("Why should I pay my hard-earned money
to support welfare chiselers?"), or it may surface in more subtle
ways, such as our tendency to think of aid to the poor as "hand-
outs." This term is one that we seldom apply to other forms of
government aid—for example, the tax deduction for interest
payments on my house, the subsidized loans for your children
in college, or the business person's deductions for expensive
lunches with drinks. This "handout" attitude is widespread even
within the church, and it deserves more attention than I can
devote to it here. For now it is enough to point out that this
attitude is both inconsistent and selfish. Hostility toward victims of poverty stands at odds with the biblical witness concerning God's intention for us. Consequently, each of us should
confront some hard questions: "Is that my attitude? Are my
stated reasons—whatever they may be—for opposing government action obscuring a loveless judgment of others?"

Some of us may answer "No." Our discomfort with the role
of government may stem from the wholly laudable concern of

wanting to help in the most effective way. After all, if we want to alleviate hunger, shouldn't we put our time and money into direct assistance—say, contributing to our church's relief agency or volunteering in a local soup kitchen. We *know* that these efforts are helpful—and aren't they more useful than trying to change government policies that may or may not eventually benefit people who are hungry? Direct assistance seems concrete and measurable compared to the uncertainties of public policy.

However, such discomfort with the role of government often reflects a disdain of the political process, a disdain that is widespread even among those who *want* to alleviate hunger. It is the feeling that one is "above" politics. Such disdain is self-righteous and self-defeating as well as loveless. It is self-righteous because it masquerades as moral superiority. It is self-defeating because it abdicates power. And because it disparages a means ordained by God for doing good, it is loveless. Disdain for the political process is all of these, no matter how saintly its disguise.

The Case for Government Action

In this chapter I want to argue the need for both private assistance *and* public action through government. One without the other will lead to failed efforts. Each deserves the finest commitment that we can offer, because each is a vital part of our Christian service. We face not an *either/or* but a *both/and* situation.

On my occasional trips abroad I have seen some of the work that is being done by groups such as Catholic Relief Services, Church World Service, Lutheran World Relief, World Relief Corporation, and World Vision. I can testify that it is highly effective. The same can be said of most of the work of major private agencies engaged in relief and development. Dollars contributed for such work make a big difference in the lives of countless people, and if Christians in the United States could see what that work does, their contributions would multiply. But even increased contributions would not reduce the importance of Christians getting government leaders to take more effective action against hunger.

Similarly, I have been deeply touched—as almost anyone would be—to see the work that is being done quietly and without fanfare across the land in soup kitchens and food pantries that feed people who have nowhere else to turn. If more Christians could see this work and come into contact with those whose lives it lifts beyond some level of pain, this work too would greatly expand. But a better private response would not alter the need for public responsibility in this area either.

I do not question the value of private assistance. But I want to stress the important role of government and the role of Christians in relation to government. Using the issue of hunger as my primary example, I will present four basic arguments for public intervention. None is an argument against private voluntary assistance. Each indicates why private assistance by itself is not enough.

1. As a national and international problem, hunger requires a national and international commitment.

While preparing this chapter, I thought of the Reverend Larry Rice, who founded and directs the New Life Evangelistic Center in St. Louis and East St. Louis. Larry began a ministry as an evangelist to poor people in St. Louis, but almost immediately he became immersed in companion efforts to obtain desperately needed food, clothing, and shelter for people who had nowhere else to turn. He started several distribution centers and shelters for the homeless. Larry knows the importance of direct assistance and gets Christians to help provide it. But he also knows the importance of getting the public to see and exercise its responsibility through the government.

I called Larry to talk to him about that side of the picture, but he wasn't at the Center. It was winter, and he was sitting in a large corrugated box in front of city hall as part of an extended vigil calling attention to the plight of the homeless and calling upon city officials to establish a shelter for them.

A couple of weeks later I managed to reach Larry at a pay phone a few feet away from his temporary "office" outside of city hall. "Why are you calling on city officials to provide shelter for the homeless?" I asked. "Aren't you asking the government to do what Christians should be doing?"

"Not at all," Larry replied. "We're asking for both voluntary and government action. If there's no community-wide responsibility, government becomes the representative of the well-to-do and can't identify with the poor. The result is not neutrality, but actions that are diametrically opposed to the needs of hungry and homeless people. We need acts of mercy, but we also need justice."

Voluntary charitable aid and direct personal involvement on the part of Christians are needed more than ever in today's world. But voluntary assistance, precisely because it is voluntary, is also limited and inconsistent. Support for it pours in when the television networks suddenly "discover" a famine that has been going on for more than a year. But contributions subside when the famine is no longer deemed newsworthy, even though malnutrition continues and the arduous work of rehabilitating land, villages, and people cries out for long-term development aid. This is especially true in Africa, a continent that would face a food crisis even if it had not been ravaged by famine, because it is the one region of the world where per-capita food production has been declining for more than two decades. As the African famine illustrates, we are creatures of the media. The ability of private voluntary organizations to raise money for their work is directly related to media coverage, which is regrettably fickle and usually focuses on short-term crises. Partly because news coverage is capricious, so is our private assistance.

When the incidence of hunger and poverty in the United States began increasing sharply in the early 1980s, churches throughout the country responded. Soup kitchens and food pantries multiplied because the number of people seeking emergency provisions soared. The response was impressive, but even so, it did not keep up with the need, which grew as unemployment swelled and assistance programs for the poor were slashed to help pay for the arms race and for tax cuts that primarily benefited the well-to-do. Furthermore, the response was uneven. Some churches did a lot, but most did little or nothing. The "distribution" of the hungry increased the challenge. Instead of being evenly distributed throughout the population, hungry people tend to be concentrated in ghettos and slums and depressed rural areas, where the churches are financially least well-situated to help.

All of this argues that hunger and poverty, along with many other basic social problems, are in the last analysis the concern of the entire nation and require that voluntary and local efforts be undergirded by national commitments. This need for national involvement in no way diminishes the importance of direct personal involvement or of indirect involvement through financial support of voluntary efforts. These efforts will remain essential, but they do not replace public responsibility.

2. The scale of assistance needed and often the speed with which it is needed require government action.

Small is beautiful, but it is *small.* Unfortunately, hunger is so massive, so widespread, that large-scale interventions are inescapable if we are going to mount successful efforts to reduce and gradually eliminate hunger. This does not detract from the vital and increasing role of private voluntary organizations. But voluntary efforts are not enough.

I write these lines a few weeks after a "Hands Across America" event attracted five million participants and sought to raise $100 million for the hungry and homeless of this nation. I confess that my feelings about the event are mixed. I feel ambivalent because I know that most of the folks who lined up to hold hands would never think of contacting a member of Congress about hunger. Furthermore, as columnist George Will pointed out, $100 million is only eight-tenths of one percent of the cost for one year of one anti-poverty program: food stamps. How easy it is to feel good about being part of a big national event on hunger, yet to ignore the process for making national decisions about hunger. One hopes, of course, that many who held hands will also discover the political process, because the "hands across America" that will have a far greater impact on hungry people are those that write letters to U.S. senators and representatives. The limitations of this mammoth fund-raising event illustrate the importance of augmenting private charity with public justice.

Let me illustrate the point with another example. There are nearly nine million Lutherans nationwide, who contribute about twenty million dollars annually for relief and development through their churches' hunger appeals. By comparison, consider that a single proposal by the president or a law enacted by Congress may determine whether hundreds of millions or even billions of dollars will be allocated to combat hunger, and how that money will be used. In 1984 the Administration made a decision to reduce this country's contribution to the International Development Association of the World Bank, and Congress willingly consented. That brought about a reduction in the giving of other donor nations as well. The result was that critical funds, which had been the basis of a three-year plan for urgently needed development aid to the poorest countries in the world, were reduced by three *billion* dollars, an annual amount fifty times larger than the combined giving of nine million Lutherans. This comparison doesn't diminish the importance of contributing for private relief and development efforts. But it does underscore how self-defeating it is to neglect major policy decisions if we want people to work their way out of hunger and poverty.

In church we give to relieve hunger. But by our silence on public policy we lock people more deeply into hunger. Does this make sense?

I have visited with Mother Teresa of Calcutta, who is probably the world's most widely respected practitioner of direct assistance to the poor. She told me that she strongly supports efforts to get the U.S. government to take actions aimed at reducing hunger. In fact, late in 1984 Mother Teresa wrote a personal letter to President Reagan, asking the Administration to respond more generously to the tragic famine in Ethiopia. Mother Teresa obviously has committed her life in an extraordinary way to the poor, and she does so through direct voluntary aid. But she understands that governments also have an essential role to play.

Let's consider the African famine more carefully. During 1983, Bread for the World became increasingly alarmed over a prolonged and spreading drought that, combined with other problems, was beginning to bring on a famine of tragic proportions, especially in Ethiopia and Mozambique. The United States was providing no assistance to either country. Lack of U.S. aid stemmed from the fact that our government considered the governments of these two countries unfriendly. Both countries are controlled by Marxist governments—one-party military dictatorships—and the regime in Ethiopia is especially repressive and ruthless. These are not exactly my favorite governments. Their failed policies, in fact, also contributed extensively to the famine. But politics was not the critical issue. The issue was that millions of people were on the brink of starvation. Many were dying. And our government was doing nothing about it.

So Bread for the World members and others began writing the State Department, asking that food supplies be sent immediately to Ethiopia and Mozambique. They also wrote their members of Congress, and before long more than one-third of the House and Senate had also pressed the State Department about the lack of assistance to these countries. Finally, in October 1983, the Administration announced that it would begin sending food supplies to Ethiopia, although at this time the amounts were relatively small.

As soon as Congress reconvened in January 1984, citizen advocates began pushing hard for emergency aid to African countries affected by the drought and faced with critical food shortages. By this time the United Nations listed two dozen such African countries and indicated that at least 150 million people were affected (though not all were starving). Bread for the World members helped mobilize a campaign of letters, calls, and visits to U.S. senators and representatives, seeking action long before the famine came to wide public attention through television network coverage. Partly as a result of this effort, Congress appropriated $150 million for emergency food aid plus $17 million for transportation and other nonfood assistance. The action fell far short of meeting the need in Africa; nevertheless, it provided food to millions of stricken people that year. And it paved the way for more massive assistance in 1985.

Bread for the World gives no direct assistance, but we worked closely with private voluntary agencies on the African crisis. These agencies were indispensable sources of information for us, and they were eager for us to mobilize our membership network so that public support could be generated to obtain congressional action. They knew from the extent and severity of the famine that large-scale and immediate government assistance was absolutely essential. They realized that they could not respond adequately to the massive need that was developing. So these agencies—precisely the ones engaged in direct voluntary aid—became the most eloquent advocates of emergency governmental aid to the famine victims. In flagging the need for wider public intervention, the agencies were fulfilling one of their most vital responsibilities as credible on-the-scene participants.

Those who argue that government action is inappropriate

might consider this question: Should starving Africans—or
hungry people anywhere—be expected to wait until we Christians are able and willing to respond privately on a scale that
meets their needs for survival? To say that they should is to
consign them to misery and death.

**3. Private aid and government action often reinforce one an-
other and are needed in combination.**

The African famine of the mid-1980s illustrates this point
clearly. Private voluntary agencies at work in Africa sought U.S.
government emergency aid not only because the famine was so
widespread but because they knew that government action was
necessary to enable them to carry out their own work. The reason is that almost all of the food distributed by private U.S.
agencies overseas comes from the U.S. government. These commodities are donated to the agencies by our government, which
also reimburses the agencies for most of the freight costs to ship
these supplies where they are needed. That is why private agencies can promise their donors that each dollar contributed to
them results in several dollars' worth of food sent to hungry
people. The arrangement is a sensible, effective way for the government and private agencies to join forces to help desperate
people. There is no point in praising and supporting private
efforts while at the same time crippling such efforts through
public neglect.

**4. Many decisions exceed the grasp of voluntary agencies and
can be made only by the government.**

After Watergate conspirator Charles Colson became a Christian, he started Prison Fellowship Ministries in response to three
acute needs that he became aware of during his imprisonment.
The first two had to do with private voluntary activities: the
need to proclaim the gospel to prisoners and to nurture them in
the church of Jesus Christ, and the need to help local churches
minister to prisoners and ex-prisoners and their families. But
the third need was different: the need for a better criminal justice
system. A private voluntary organization does not decide how
the criminal justice system will function; that is the government's role. So Prison Fellowship Ministries established Justice
Fellowship to work on criminal justice reform. Justice Fellowship involves Christians in citizen advocacy to improve the role

of government in dealing with offenders and their victims. Without such an effort, the ministry of Christians in this area of concern would be severely impaired, to everyone's detriment.

So it is with hunger. Trade, unemployment, military spending, and fiscal and monetary policies are all matters that vitally affect poor and hungry people worldwide. But private agencies cannot make such policies. Only governments can.

Africa illustrates this point all too well. Most food-deficit countries of Africa are in deep financial debt, partly because of such factors as the oil price hikes of the 1970s, the worldwide recession that ensued, and some ill-advised economic decisions made in many of these countries. But their financial woes are also partly attributable to U.S. economic policies such as high interest rates brought about in part by our huge federal deficits. In 1985, for example, it was estimated that payments that lower-income countries in sub-Saharan Africa would have to make on their debts would gobble up as much as 40 percent of their total export earnings. This burden of debt makes it exceedingly difficult for extremely poor countries to finance the kind of development that would enable them to work their way out of hunger and poverty. And there is not much that private agencies or private aid can do, but there is a great deal that our government can do about such indebtedness.

Many countries in Africa are dependent upon one or two crops or minerals for most of their export earnings. Unfortunately, over the years the terms of trade—what they can buy in relation to the coffee or peanuts or copper that they sell—have turned against them, so it takes increasingly more coffee, peanuts, or copper to buy the same essential imports. These countries need to diversify their exports. They need to process more of their own raw materials and sell more finished products abroad. Otherwise, many of their people will never have the opportunity to employ and feed themselves adequately. But selling abroad requires open markets. Consequently, the trade policies of the United States and other prosperous nations play an important role in determining whether or not hungry people are able to work their way out of hunger and poverty. But private agencies cannot determine these policies. The government does that.

One reason that markets in the United States are not more

open to competing products from developing countries is our high unemployment rate. We fear the adverse impact of imported products on our jobs and industries. As a result, unemployment in the United States causes hunger and poverty not only here but abroad as well. However, U.S. economic policies, which have a great bearing on our unemployment rate, are not established by private individuals, agencies, or companies. They are established by the president and the Congress of this nation.

Consider military spending. Between 1973 and 1983, Africa—the last place on earth able to afford it—made a tenfold increase in its spending on military imports, from $470 million to $4.8 billion. United States policy has encouraged this. One can argue about whether or not the emphasis on military hardware is warranted, but there is hardly any doubt that for economically strapped countries, money spent on the military is money that cannot be used to meet basic human needs. We have witnessed the same phenomenon in our own country. As military spending soared during the 1980s, funds for programs to assist the poor began drying up. More people fell below the poverty line, and more went hungry. This relationship between "guns and hunger" is what prompted President Dwight D. Eisenhower to say, "Every gun that is made, every warship launched, every rocket fired signifies, in the final sense, a theft from those who hunger and are not fed, those who are cold and are not clothed."[2]

Debt, trade, unemployment, and military spending illustrate my larger point that the federal government, and the federal government alone, is responsible for many decisions that bear heavily on hunger. It is not simply because the government can give aid on a much larger scale than private agencies, but because the very nature of many key hunger issues removes them from private hands and places them in the hands of the federal government. Either we attempt to influence government policy on such issues, or we stand on the sidelines and watch.

There is much to commend in voluntary assistance. But we also need to recognize its limitations—and its temptations. Voluntary aid (charity is still a good word for it) often brings with

2. Eisenhower, "The Chance for Peace," an address before the American Society of Newspaper Editors on April 16, 1953.

it the satisfaction of providing some measurable benefit to another. It is more concrete and more clearly grasped than the complexities of public policy. It is emotionally satisfying, as well as useful, to serve in a soup kitchen or to sponsor a child overseas. But the danger is that, feeling satisfied, we never ask *why* people are mired in hunger and poverty. What are the causes of their hunger? How can we do more than meet their immediate need? How can we help to bring about changed conditions that will enable hungry people to become independent and contribute through their own skill and labor to a world less plagued by hunger?

The Need for a National Commitment

The nature of hunger as a national and global concern, the amount of assistance needed, the link between private and government aid, and the type of decisions that affect hunger all argue persuasively for a public role in the issue of hunger. That role is inevitable. Our federal government cannot avoid making decisions that in one way or another have enormous impact on hungry people. The only question is whether the impact will reduce hunger or bury more people. If we Christians, who *do* care when others go hungry, separate ourselves from such decisions, we turn them over to leaders who, probably through ignorance or neglect more than malicious intent, will not have the suffering of hungry people in mind. And we can expect such decisions to contribute to the continuation of hunger. We have no reason to expect anything else.

The basic direction of this argument applies to a great many other issues as well. Because public decisions can profoundly affect people's lives, Christians have reason to take an active interest in them and become part of the decision-making process. Hunger is a particularly good example of why that is so, but by no means the only example.

To be fair, over the past several decades this nation has tried to address world hunger. But our efforts have been erratic. We have never made the elimination of hunger a major priority. In view of the commanding role that the United States plays in the world economy and of the advantages of our enormous wealth, advanced technology, and numerous human resources, it is not acceptable that Christians here tolerate, virtually unchallenged, the continuation of so massive and unnecessary a human tragedy as world hunger.

"Unnecessary" is the correct word, and it casts the issue in an entirely different light than that in which it is usually seen. Hunger is not new. The world has known hunger as long as human history has been recorded. What is new about hunger is that it is no longer necessary, a statement that can be accurately applied only to the last several decades. Humankind has the technical knowledge to eradicate hunger. Doing so would be a massive undertaking, but it would be possible. That is why former West German Chancellor Willy Brandt says, "Morally it makes no difference whether someone is killed in a war or dies from hunger as a result of our neglect."[3] We have the capability to eliminate hunger, but we lack the will to do it. I do not say *merely* the will, because there is nothing mere about it. The will is more crucial and more stubbornly evasive than the necessary technology. And the will must not only be expressed in millions of individual efforts but translated into national policy decisions as well.

The need for political will was underscored in November 1974 when the United Nations convened a World Food Conference in response to worldwide food shortages and regional famines. United States Secretary of State Henry Kissinger proposed, and the conference resolved, "that within a decade no child will go to bed hungry." However, the decade ended with more, not fewer, children going to bed hungry. The United Nations Children's Fund (UNICEF) reports that each day more than forty thousand young children die from malnutrition and infection— a number that, tallied annually, exceeds the entire U.S. population of children five years old and under. Why did we fail? Kissinger left no doubt about that in his own speech. "The profound promise of our era," he said, "is that for the first time we may have the technical capacity to free mankind from the scourge of hunger. Therefore, today we must proclaim a bold objective— that within a decade no child will go to bed hungry, that no family will fear for its next day's bread and that no human

3. Brandt, in the introduction to *North-South: A Program for Survival* (Cambridge: MIT Press, 1980), p. 16.

being's future and capacities will be stunted by malnutrition." He went on to urge joint action "to regain control over our shared destiny. If we do not act boldly, disaster will result from a failure of will." But bold action was noticeably absent in the ensuing decade. The rhetoric was breathtaking, but it reflected no national commitment on the part of this country or its leaders. In short, to use Kissinger's words, there was "a failure of will."

Following the World Food Conference, President Gerald R. Ford commissioned the National Academy of Sciences to study and advise the nation regarding ways in which it could contribute technologically to the elimination of hunger. A panel of fifteen hundred distinguished scientists collaborated on a six-volume report that was released in 1976. Perhaps the most striking conclusion of these scientists was that because we have or can anticipate having the technology to overcome hunger, the key factor is political will: "If there is the political will in this country and abroad . . . it should be possible to overcome the worst aspects of widespread hunger and malnutrition within one generation."[4] A bipartisan commission appointed by President Jimmy Carter subsequently underscored the same point and recommended that the elimination of hunger become the primary focus of U.S. relations with developing countries—one more report that has been celebrated with neglect.

This lack of political will presents a great challenge to U.S. Christians. We can use the gift of citizenship to help get our national leaders to make decisions that can turn an effort against hunger into a national commitment. Not that the United States can by itself overcome world hunger—not by a long shot. But we can—and we should—take the lead on this issue and invite other nations, both rich and poor, to enter into a partnership toward that end.

In future efforts against hunger, voluntary assistance will become increasingly important. But such assistance would be enormously enhanced, not diminished, by a national political commitment to help end hunger. We cannot ignore the role that the president and the Congress play in determining national

4. *World Food and Nutrition Study: The Potential Contributions of Research* (Washington: National Academy of Sciences, 1977), p. 5.

commitments on matters that range from education to space exploration. In the fight to abolish slavery in the nineteenth century and in the struggle to establish civil rights in this century, countless individual sacrifices and acts of courage paved the way. Voluntary efforts and citizen advocacy, seemingly futile at times, were indispensable in changing the political climate. But the highest government authorities had to declare new national policies before real changes could emerge. That is the role of political leadership in shaping national values and declaring national goals on hunger and many other issues.

I am sometimes asked, "If you had to single out one thing that would do most to move us toward the elimination of hunger, what would that be?" My answer: a national commitment to end hunger. Not just in rhetoric but in reality. Once that commitment is made, a host of policy decisions consistent with it could be enacted. The commitment is the key. This being the case, the work cut out for us is to build step-by-step on policy decisions that can move us toward such a commitment.

Chapter 4
Finding the Right Policies

> *People are always extolling the man of principles; but I think the superior man is one who knows that he must find his way in a maze of principles.*
>
> —Justice Oliver Wendell Holmes

> *I speak not of forcible annexation for that cannot be thought of. That by our code of morals would be criminal aggression.*
>
> —President William McKinley prior to the U.S. annexation of the Philippines

> *I am not ashamed to tell you gentlemen that I went on my knees and prayed to Almighty God for light and guidance more than one night. And one night it came to me this way— that there was nothing left for us to do but to take them all, and to educate the Filipinos, and uplift and civilize them, and by God's grace do the very best we could do by them, as our fellowmen for whom Christ also died.*
>
> —President William McKinley after the forcible annexation of the Philippines

I remember when I was trying to figure out what God wanted me to undertake as my vocation in life. Journalism? Law? Theology? I knew something about journalism from my father's profession of writing and publishing, and from working on my brother's newspaper. I knew almost nothing about the legal profession, though that seemed to me a plausible springboard for Christian service. And I had a pretty good idea of what pastoral ministry was like because I had grown up in a parsonage. But what work did God want me to do? There was no proof passage in the Bible to answer that question, no writing in the sky, no dream, no voice from heaven. It was an agonizing struggle, a time for soul-searching and intense thinking. Finally, with the help of some guidance from others, a bit of instinct, and many prayers, I decided to prepare for the parish ministry. The choice seemed right to me, but one makes such a choice—or at least I did—seeing only a step or two ahead, knowing the decision will be subject to further testing and probing, further understanding and development, perhaps even complete revision.

Discerning God's Will

The question "How do I discern God's will?" is one that we face in many different situations, and finding an agenda for policy action is no exception. The quest for God's will brings us to the toughest part of our assignment. Everything else is easy by comparison. How do we discern God's will on matters that rarely lend themselves to absolute clarity? In Chapter Two I noted that the Bible offers us no Christian economics, no political blueprint. There are no straight lines connecting faith and a policy agenda, only indirect lines. And the indirect lines, precisely because they are indirect, do not invite certainty.

At this point we run into a problem that none of us can avoid: bringing our own personal biases and cultural baggage into any consideration of a policy agenda. We do so inescapably. This is true no matter what our political leanings—left, right, or center. We are not inclined to perceive the extent to which personal and cultural factors influence our opinions. We are prone to assume that our viewpoints are based upon sound moral principles and persuasive evidence. Even when we go by hunches, as we often do, each of us is disposed to think that his or her hunches are close to God's intentions. Like Charlie Brown on the pitching mound, we're so sincere—how can we be wrong? So we may feel that we have divine sanction for positions that simply reflect secular values around and within us. And as a general rule, the more certain we are that we speak for God on these matters, the more apt we are to be wrong.

Fortunately, we are not left without guidance. The Bible and our Christian tradition give us a solid foundation to build on. The more carefully we build on this foundation and the more willing we are to critically examine our own views, the more likely we are to build well. In any case, Christian faith does not allow the lack of certainty to serve as an excuse for inaction. Struggle we must. And act we must.

In his second inaugural address, Abraham Lincoln revealed his profound understanding of human limitations in the quest for divine guidance, but that understanding did not prevent him from taking decisive action. The nation had gone through a terrible civil war that was almost finished. Neither side had wanted the war. Neither side had expected it to be so long or severe, Lincoln said.

> Each looked for an easier triumph, and a result less fundamental and astounding. Both read the same Bible and pray to the same God, and each invokes His aid against the other. It may seem strange that any men should dare to ask a just God's assistance in wringing their bread from the sweat of other men's faces, but let us judge not, that we be not judged. The prayers of both could not be answered. That of neither has been answered fully. The Almighty has His own purposes.

"Fondly do we hope, fervently do we pray, that this mighty scourge of war may speedily pass away," Lincoln went on. "Yet, if God wills that it continue . . . as was said three thousand years ago, so still it must be said, 'The judgments of the Lord are true and righteous altogether.' " Lincoln concluded his address by summoning the nation to move forward with a spirit of compassion: "With malice toward none, with charity for all, with firmness in the right as God gives us to see the right, let us strive on to finish the work we are in, to bind up the nation's wounds."

Even though he had the end of slavery and the preservation of the Union in mind, Lincoln was not willing to fully identify his aims and those of the North with God's will or stand in judgment of his southern adversaries. His humility is apparent in the face of so costly a struggle. Lincoln saw the ambiguity of the situation and the need for forgiveness. He also saw the need for action.

No Leap from Faith to Public Policy

Conceding inevitable uncertainty, how do we develop an agenda for action? It helps to identify the following three categories:

1. Revealed principles
2. Derived moral principles
3. Public policy positions

The further we move beyond revealed principles of faith, the more we encounter uncertainty. Public policy positions are more subject to misjudgment than derived moral principles, although misjudgment is possible at any point. I have listed these three categories, which we can also think of as steps or stages, in a logical sequence. But it rarely happens that we work through stages one and two before considering the issues of stage three. Ordinarily we find ourselves grappling with a policy issue that has for some reason attracted our interest. Even so, the three categories can provide a framework for our thinking and help us consider issues from a Christian perspective.

We approach *all three* categories from the standpoint of faith— that is, from the standpoint of God's great love for us in Christ. From this flows all of our thinking and doing, including the way we are neighbors to others through civic stewardship.

1. *Revealed principles.* These are fundamental principles, drawn from the Bible, that express core teachings of faith. We should not imagine a wooden list of things to believe, all of equal importance. Rather, the principles must be seen as they emerge from the central biblical themes of creation, redemption, and sanctification. It is not always obvious whether or not a statement fits this category. The mere fact that a statement comes from the Bible does not make it a fundamental principle on which to build social ethics. (An example is the apostle Paul's advice that women should keep their heads covered in public worship.) The following statements illustrate what I mean by revealed principles that express core teachings of faith. They represent only a limited sampling, a few of many such principles:

- We have been created in the image of God.
- The earth is the Lord's.
- God rescued his people from slavery and made a covenant with them.
- In Christ God was reconciling the world to himself.
- You shall not kill.
- You shall not steal.
- By nature we are sinful.
- Human life is immeasurably precious.
- We are accountable to God for the way we treat others.

Some of these principles are more basic than others. Some derive from others. But all are unmistakably grounded in the Bible. Each has wider moral implications, including many that apply to hunger and poverty. They provide a few of the foundation stones on which we can build other moral principles (stage two) that in turn guide us when we consider policy positions (stage three).

2. *Derived moral principles.* These middle principles stand between revealed principles and public policy positions. It is a great mistake to imagine that we can simply leap from faith in Jesus Christ or from some basic affirmation of faith to a political agenda. This misguided idea leads to all sorts of mischief. In *First Lady from Plains,* Rosalynn Carter tells of crossing in front of a long line of women at a shopping center who held in the palms of their hands printed cards that said, "You don't love Jesus."

"I do love Jesus," Mrs. Carter told some of them.

"If you loved Jesus, you wouldn't support the ERA!" was their reply.[1]

In this situation some unacknowledged assumptions and middle principles were involved, but these were brushed aside as though they did not exist. Acknowledging them would have subjected the issue to more scrutiny and less certainty—probably the last thing these women wanted. No, it was enough for them to know and proclaim that Mrs. Carter didn't love Jesus because she supported the ERA. That their arrogance and loveless judgment violated the teachings of Jesus seems not to have occurred to them. They wanted to draw a straight line from faith to public policy and condemn as faithless those who disagreed with their stance. If you substitute Nancy Reagan for Rosalynn Carter and reverse the position on the ERA, the story illustrates the same point.

A direct leap from faith to policy prescriptions is often made by Christians who support or oppose a nuclear arms freeze, abortion, prayer in the public schools, and a host of other issues. The feeling of certainty that such a leap provides is self-deceptive and dangerous. When a policy prescription is seen to come directly from revealed truth, prayer, or faith, and to represent

1. Carter, *First Lady from Plains* (Boston: Houghton Mifflin, 1984), pp. 335-36.

the only morally upright opinion, there is no longer room for consideration of contrary evidence or other points of view—and the result is frequently outrage over the opposition's perversity. This undermines the civility that makes democracy possible. A more humble and a more biblical approach is necessary, one that can see the distance between fundamental principles, about which we can have the certainty of faith, and policy prescriptions, which are inevitably flawed. As Richard John Neuhaus has pointed out in *Christian Faith and Public Policy,* "We do not have a word from the Lord on whether the hungry children of the poor should be fed through a food stamp program or through a guaranteed annual income. We do have a word from the Lord against a system that allows them to go hungry."[2]

In *Crime and Its Victims* Daniel Van Ness makes much the same point with regard to the way in which the Old Testament law informs our understanding of criminal punishment:

> We do not look at the Law with the expectation that we can or should enact it directly through our legislatures. Instead we derive its significance for us through a series of steps:
> 1. Understand its context.
> 2. Ask ourselves how theology understands and informs the passages we are examining.
> 3. Look at the Law itself, together with comparable passages of Scripture where the underlying purposes or principles are more explicit, as well as contemporaneous extrabiblical resources.
> 4. Identify the principles behind the particular passages we are studying. We are looking for principles which lie between the general theological understanding of "justice," for example, and the specific, concrete regulations that appear in the Law.
>
> This gives us a way to study the one time when God instructed a nation in how it should deal with what we now call criminal cases (among other aspects of national life), and take from that study principles we can use to critique and modify our own system of justice.[3]

Middle principles have to be developed with great care. For example, by focusing exclusively on the faith-based principle that "the earth is the Lord's," one could develop moral princi-

---

2. Neuhaus, *Christian Faith and Public Policy: Thinking and Acting in the Courage of Uncertainty* (Minneapolis: Augsburg, 1977), p. 52.

3. Van Ness, *Crime and Its Victims: What We Can Do* (Downers Grove, Ill.: InterVarsity Press, 1986), pp. 107-8.

ples that ignore the right of private ownership. This in turn might lead to policy prescriptions totally hostile to free enterprise. Or one could derive from the commandment "Thou shalt not steal" the principle that personal property rights are absolute and inviolable. That principle in turn might serve as the basis for a political agenda featuring the most rigid protection for property, an agenda opposing, let us say, any type of income, property, or inheritance tax, or justifying slavery. The problem in each instance is a failure to view a basic principle of faith within the larger biblical framework. That framework includes both the assumption that "the earth is the Lord's" and the assumption that property rights are to be respected. Thus property rights cannot be absolute—a viewpoint buttressed by Old Testament laws that required lending without interest, forgiving monetary obligations every seventh year, allocating the tithe and harvest gleanings for the poor, and periodically restoring land to its original owners (or their descendants). As Chapter Two indicates, a great deal of biblical material sheds light on the matter of possessions in relation to justice. It allows us to derive moral principles that take into account more than one basic principle of faith. Doing so protects us to some extent against selectively using the Bible in such a way that we manipulate it to justify opinions that are rooted elsewhere.

The brief sampling of principles of faith (stage one) already provided shows us that many of them speak to the issue of hunger, some more centrally than others. From these it is possible to derive moral principles (stage two) that serve as guidelines in the construction of a policy agenda. My purpose here is not to suggest a complete set of principles but to offer a few examples.

One such principle is that we have a special responsibility, and therefore an accountability, with regard to those who are poor and hungry. (You might argue that this is a basic principle of faith rather than a derived moral principle, but for now let us err on the side of caution.) Knowing that we have a responsibility does not tell us how we are to carry it out. We do have some clues, however. One clue is that the biblical writers espouse both charity (voluntary assistance) and justice (fairness in the system). Justice in turn implies the establishment of public policies (government laws, regulations, practices) that in

combination with nongovernmental efforts assure at least some
minimal safeguards against poverty. Safeguards might include
self-help opportunities such as job training and employment for
those who are able to work, and an economic safety net providing food, shelter, and other basic necessities for those who cannot or should not work. In these few sentences I have sketched
a set of related moral principles, derived from basic principles
of faith, about which there might be something approaching
widespread agreement among U.S. Christians.

Another derived moral principle, one that Bread for the World
has stressed, is the right to food. The right to food is implicit in
the right to life, a biblical principle that finds expression in the
Declaration of Independence, which calls life an "unalienable
right" endowed by the Creator. The right to food is grounded in
the extraordinary value God assigns to human life and in the
fundamental obligations God places on us with regard to the
lives of others. Because food is essential to human life, opportunity to obtain it is a right. The term "right," it should be noted,
emerges from the language of law. It is not a term that appropriately describes our relationship to God, who grants life not
as a right but as a gift. However, the term is useful in establishing
ground rules for human behavior because it asserts that people
do have some basic and specific claims to justice in their deal-
ings with each other.

The right to food is an unusual example in one respect. It is
a derived moral principle that also became a public policy objective and was adopted by Congress in 1976. (See Appendix
II.) The reason for making it a policy goal was to get public and
congressional support for a declaration of intent regarding hunger, and in doing so to lay the groundwork for other policy
actions. The principle did in fact serve that purpose. Ordinarily,
however, we do not think of moral principles as objectives for
a policy agenda.

It is in this middle area of derived moral principles, as well
as in the framing of specific positions on policy issues (stage
three), that we struggle to determine an appropriate role for government in distinction from roles that may more suitably belong
to the family, private enterprise, or other nongovernmental institutions. All can promote the common good, but divine revelation seldom shows us how they best do so in relation to one

another on specific issues. Nor does human experience yield self-evident answers. In grappling with the question of appropriate government roles, as with other issues, we must continually examine and re-examine human experience in the light of revealed principles of faith as we develop moral guidelines.

3. *Public policy positions.* When we work on policy proposals, we have every reason to do so with modesty and courage. Both modesty and courage are called for because we need to take action on matters concerning which we cannot claim certainty.

Let me comment first on the need for modesty.

At the stage of policy positions, we begin applying biblical and moral principles. We do so without the benefit of detailed instructions from God. We have to offer specific prescriptions that require a reasonably accurate reading of complex social problems and a fair sense of the probable impact of a policy if it is adopted. What is required, therefore, is not only fidelity to Christian moral principles but sound analysis of policy issues. But Christians have no inside track on sound analysis, no special revelation that gives them quick solutions to tangled social problems.

It would be an exceptional reader (exceptionally inexperienced or exceptionally stubborn) who could not think back and recall having at least a few policy opinions that now seem quite wrongheaded or at least questionable. When I served a parish on Manhattan's Lower East Side, I got involved in housing issues. A majority of the old tenements there were under rent control. The law permitted a 15 percent increase in rent when new tenants moved into an apartment, so rents varied wildly, with no particular correspondence to the quality or size of the apartments. Building code violations abounded. Often buildings were in bad repair, apartments poorly maintained, and heat and basic services erratic. It seemed to me that landlords took advantage of tenants more often than not. Having visited families in run-down apartments—the plaster cracked and full of holes, the windows broken, no heat in the dead of winter—I had some sense of what neighborhood people had to put up with. I favored rent control because, uneven as the outcome was, it gave vulnerable people at least *some* protection against rent gouging in a tight housing market. But over time my perspective changed. As the years went by, more and more buildings burned down and were abandoned. Fires were rife in the neighborhood, and the word was that many of them occurred because landlords could do better collecting insurance than collecting rent. Without rent control, rents would have soared, and people would have suffered more. On the other hand, burned-out and torn-down buildings robbed them of housing, too. Without rent control, many of those buildings would have been saved. In retrospect, I'm not sure I was right about rent control. I'm not certain I was wrong, either, but I suspect that I was.

In that case I erred on the side of favoring a government intervention that I now think was unwarranted. An example of the opposite kind of mistake comes from Senator Ernest F. Hollings (D-S.C.), who as governor of South Carolina refused to admit that the state had a hunger problem. "I was a victim of hunger myopia," he later wrote. "I can't say that I really saw hunger until I went traveling with a Catholic nun, Sister Anthony, in January 1968." Sister Anthony thought Hollings, an active Protestant, meant well and could learn, so she invited him to visit some families in Charleston, South Carolina. Hollings remembers the trip well: "Before we had gone a block, I was miserable. . . . I began to understand . . . that hunger was real, and it existed in hundreds of humans in my own home city. I saw what all America needs to see. The hungry are not able-bodied men, sitting around drunk and lazy on welfare. They are children. They are abandoned women, or the crippled or the aged."[4] Hollings' views had been shaped in part by political convenience, but the evidence prompted him to change his mind, and he became a supporter of legislation to end hunger in the United States.

If personal experience does not give us sufficient reason for caution, consider the experience of the churches—perhaps that of your own religious denomination. The churches have certainly played a crucial and on the whole a highly positive role in the shaping of our nation. But their record on social issues is not uncheckered. Several examples prove the point. When life insurance first appeared, many religious bodies vigorously opposed it, claiming that it was the casting of one's lot with mam-

4. Hollings, *The Case against Hunger* (New York: Cowles, 1970), p. 22.

mon and showed a lack of trust in God. In its day, slavery was widely defended within the churches and was tacitly or officially sanctioned by some. Subsequently, segregation and the denial of civil rights to blacks came to be widely accepted by church bodies. The position of women in society and in the church has undergone enormous change over the years. Prior to and at the outset of each world war, U.S. churches were strongly isolationist, but once this country declared war, the churches could not beat the drums loud enough in support of the war effort. I do not mean to be overly critical. Each of these issues was complex and evoked controversy within the church. But when the churches jumped into the arena of opinion, they did not always land on their feet, and on some important issues they later reversed their opinion. It is reasonable to suspect that churches, like individuals, take positions that are frequently more affected by secular influences than by theology.

I have stressed the need for a healthy dose of humility in taking policy positions because there is such a widespread tendency to assume certainty on these matters. Let me now emphasize that taking no action at all is equally as deplorable as acting with unwarranted certainty. Therefore, *courage* is also needed.

It is not hard to understand why people are instinctively uneasy about getting involved in citizen advocacy. "If it's that difficult and uncertain, count me out!" might seem a sensible response. It is a safe response in the sense that it is risk-free. On the other hand, life is not risk-free, and when Jesus calls us to follow him, he does not extend a risk-free invitation. In the end, the "safe" approach—doing nothing—is a vote for evil to prevail, which is hardly the purpose of discipleship. In the parable of the talents (in Matthew 25), Jesus condemns the servant whose cowardice led him to bury rather than invest the money that his master had entrusted to him. That servant took the risk-free approach, which in the end turned out to embody the highest danger of all. It is obvious that the risk-free, do-nothing approach to public policy on hunger can only consign hundreds of millions of people to extreme hardship and premature death. But on other issues, too, doing nothing is a loveless response, a vote for evil to prevail.

A Few Examples of Constructive Action

Action on public policy is imperative. Consider our criminal justice system. During recent years our prison population has grown at an alarming rate, and today the United States has more than half a million prisoners. Our prisons are overcrowded, and we cannot seem to build new ones fast enough. California alone is spending more than a billion dollars on new prison facilities. As a nation, we do not present a healthy picture regarding crime and punishment. To our own great shame and to the detriment of all, Christians have largely avoided this area of ministry. One solution that Justice Fellowship has been urging strikes me as uncommonly sensible. Instead of locking up nonviolent offenders—which means enormous cost to the public and often results in the personal destruction of the offenders—have them make restitution to their victims.[5] There is biblical precedent for this kind of punishment. It fits biblically derived principles. And it seems to work in the states that are trying it. The solution is not perfect, and it is not comprehensive: it deals only with some offenses and offenders. But it illustrates that even in areas as complex as criminal justice, we have opportunity to work for public policy reforms that can benefit many people.

Several targets on the policy agenda of Bread for the World illustrate the same point.

1. I have already mentioned the African famine of the mid-1980s and our work in helping to get emergency aid approved. Because the famine was so widespread and the need for emergency aid so well documented by observers, including private voluntary agencies at work in the stricken countries, this was a clearer case than most for a policy position that fit moral guidelines and offered an almost self-evident course of action. But even this case was not without its challenges. Many problems concerning transportation and distribution had to be worked out, and Bread for the World differed sharply with the Administration and some members of Congress regarding the extent to which food could be effectively distributed. We pushed for much higher amounts than the Administration requested, and the action that Congress took resulted in amounts that came out some-

5. Van Ness, *Crime and Its Victims*, chaps. 8-10, 12.

where between. In retrospect, most (but not all) observers agree that U.S. emergency supplies were fully utilized and that more could have been used. No judgments made were flawless. But the fact remains that without action, millions of people would have starved to death.

2. Because per-capita food production in Africa has been declining for more than two decades, the food crisis there reaches far beyond the famine, which is merely the tip of the iceberg. Long-term measures must overcome economic stagnation, encourage slower population growth, and reverse trends in soil erosion, deforestation, desertification, and, above all, food production. If these goals are to be accomplished, a wide range of initiatives is needed, including policy reforms within African countries regarding the production and distribution of food, more and better-targeted aid, and better market incentives for the small-scale producers who make up the great majority of the population in Africa.

While assessing other longer-term solutions, Bread for the World sought funding for a special African account within the International Fund for Agricultural Development (IFAD). IFAD specializes—with impressive success—in helping subsistence-level and other small-scale farmers produce more food. For half the cost of sending a ton of food to Africa for famine relief, IFAD projects can enable such landholders to produce an additional ton of food each year for the rest of their lifetimes. IFAD also has persuaded governments to remove restrictions such as cheap-food policies so that the free market might offer farmers more incentive to increase production. The IFAD legislation is only one step toward a long-term solution in Africa. But it does respond to widespread evidence concerning needs in Africa and what has been shown to work well in relation to those needs. The main obstacle in this case was getting funds appropriated for IFAD's African account at a time when foreign aid and many other programs were being sharply cut.

3. In 1983 the Administration obtained congressional approval for its Caribbean Basin Initiative, a package of measures designed to bring not only aid but trade and investment incentives to that region of the Americas. Bread for the World worried that business incentives might mean that land currently used for local food production would be used instead to produce

goods for export sales abroad. That would enhance the incomes of a few while increasing malnutrition among many. So Bread for the World drafted a "land for food" amendment that provided safeguards against such an outcome as well as against the further consolidation of land holdings by large landowners. The legislation passed, and the following year a modified version of the same amendment was included in trade legislation that applied to developing countries outside the Caribbean Basin. The land-for-food provision broke new ground in trade legislation by including for the first time a protection against malnutrition. The idea has potential benefits and poses little if any risk of an adverse impact.

4. You may complain that I am offering examples of policy positions that sound too much like "motherhood" issues that almost anyone would be inclined to support (though in fact we had to fight hard for each of them). So let me mention a major legislative proposal that was designed to be controversial: the Human Needs and World Security Bill of 1984. This bill offered a package of measures under a unifying theme: If we respond to basic human needs in developing countries, we will also be attending to legitimate concerns for peace and security. The underlying analysis was that as a nation we have tended to ignore hunger and poverty in developing countries until a political crisis occurs; then we often rush in with a military solution even though the problems may be social and economic in origin. Central America illustrates this reaction, and in different ways so did Iran and Indochina. The legislation that Bread for the World proposed was a response to the fact that over a three-year period our military and security aid to developing countries had jumped by 72 percent, while food and development aid had leveled off. The bill sought to restore some balance by proposing increases in specific aid programs that have proven to be highly effective in directly benefiting the poorest of the poor, while attempting to prevent further increases in our military and security aid. We succeeded in obtaining most of the humanitarian aid that we sought, but we were not able to hold the line against increases in military and security aid. (We lost by a 208-207 vote in the House and a 54-46 vote in the Senate.)

The proposed freeze on increases in military and security aid moved the Human Needs and World Security Bill beyond the category of fairly simple humanitarian legislation into an area where emotions run high and analysis is fraught with sharply differing assumptions and conclusions. Should we swim in these treacherous waters? Bread for the World's board of directors decided that we should do so in this instance, not because it was self-evident that we had the right answer, but because the issue was of exceptional importance, and the most persuasive evidence, we thought, pointed in the direction of the bill.

Developing countries with extremely limited resources are deeply hurt by any unnecessary diversion of resources from basic development to military spending. Yet during the 1970s, while world military spending was soaring, the share of world military spending accounted for by developing countries rose from 17 to 22 percent. A study done for the United Nations examined the relationship between defense spending and economic growth in fifty-four developing countries. In every case, higher defense spending was accompanied by slower economic growth. The study found that each additional dollar spent on arms appeared to reduce agricultural output by an average of twenty cents.[6]

Between 1981 and 1986, the only increases in U.S. food aid to Africa came during 1984 and 1985, the two worst years of the famine. These were extraordinarily important increases, but they were temporary. Aside from that, the 15 percent increase in U.S. food and development aid from 1981 to 1986 did not quite keep up with inflation, so its real value declined. During the same years, U.S. security aid to Africa increased by 77 percent, and U.S. military sales and assistance increased by 286 percent.

Taking all of this into account, we concluded that the U.S. government's increased military and security aid represented a misallocation of resources that was fostering hunger abroad. So we proposed the Human Needs and World Security Bill. We were aware that our understanding might be flawed. Nevertheless, the risk of inaction seemed greater than the risk of wrong action.

6. Reported in "Defense Spending, Economic Structure, and Growth: Evidence among Countries and over Time," by Riccardo Faini, Patricia Annez, and Lance Taylor, in *Economic Development and Cultural Change* (Chicago: University of Chicago Press, 1984), pp. 487-98.

5. Food stamps are also controversial. Over the years Bread for the World has supported reforms in the food-stamp program as well as efforts to reduce abuse of it and improve management in it. But we have also supported adequate funding for the program. Senate Minority Leader Bob Dole (R-Kans.) calls the food-stamp program "the most important social program since social security." The program achieved its greatest gains during the Nixon Administration, when some of the worst features of hunger in this nation were eliminated. But as a result of a subsequent recession, high unemployment, and sharp cuts in domestic programs for the poor, the hunger lines began to form again. By 1985 a nationwide study by the Physicians' Task Force on Hunger in America estimated that twenty million people go hungry two or more days a month in the United States. Food stamps are not an adequate substitute for employment and cash income, but where that is not possible, food stamps and other food-assistance programs are vital to the health and well-being of millions of families. On this issue as on others, one needs to distinguish between goals and means. The goal of reducing and eliminating hunger is consistent with revealed principles of faith and derived moral principles. The food-stamp program is not the only means for reaching that goal, and it may not be the best means, but in Bread for the World's judgment, the evidence strongly supports the importance and effectiveness of this program under present circumstances.

Avoiding Ideologies

As these and other policy goals illustrate, the best orientation is practical rather than ideological. Bread for the World starts with a fundamental human problem like hunger and then asks what steps can be taken to solve that problem. We try to avoid coming at the problem of hunger with prepackaged political or economic schemes, and concentrate instead on "what works." The approach is people-oriented and evidence-oriented rather than theory-oriented. The approach offends ideologues of both the left and the right. But it is one that attracts respect and bipartisan support in Congress, and it is able to bring about substantial, concrete benefits for hungry people. We do not have a privileged word from God regarding our selection of policy targets. We do not claim that our proposals are inarguably correct. Nor do we suggest that those who differ with us are moral outcasts.

Bread for the World opposes tyranny of every stripe. Therefore, we support human rights, the denial of which often goes hand in hand with hunger. We also respect the strengths of a free-market economy, a choice tempered by the realization that capitalism needs guidance if it is to be socially responsible. Responsible capitalism appeals to me. Free enterprise provides an impressive engine for economic growth—but an engine is not a steering wheel. Put another way, the profit motive can accomplish marvelous feats, but left entirely to its own devices, it can ride roughshod over people, with little or no respect for justice. It has, for example, extensively damaged the environment. So the public has had to intervene and through government establish rules to protect the environment. Without such intervention, greed takes over, and for the sake of immediate personal gains, long-term but unacknowledged debts are incurred that the public ultimately pays for either by living in a degraded environment or by shouldering the cost of restoring it.

Of course, free enterprise can take different forms. I like enterprise that is free enough so that all can participate in it and benefit from it. Free enterprise will be an essential part of the solution to the food crisis in Africa, for example. But that should mean, above all, the provision of opportunities for small-scale producers, not the concentration of land and profit in the hands of the few while the many waste away. This illustrates what I mean by guiding the engine of free enterprise with a steering wheel of socially responsible policies.

I am candidly stating some personal views, laying my cards on the table so you can examine them. My views, like yours, are not unbiased. They may be mistaken, and they need always to be reconsidered in the light of faith and derived moral principles as well as empirical evidence about what works and what doesn't in today's world.

We have reason to beware of ideologies, for these take us captive. Ideologies offer the attraction of breathtaking clarity. An overarching political and economic view of the world explains everything—and everything is made to fit that view. This is true whether one is a visionary of the left or the right. Inconvenient facts are brushed aside, and people are ill-served.

In Alfred Hitchcock's film *The Lady Vanishes,* the professor is confronted with evidence proving beyond a shadow of a doubt that his explanation of the case under investigation is wrong. "Nonsense," he replies. "My theory is perfectly correct. It is the facts that are misleading." Columnist David S. Broder wrote in the same vein regarding one of the nation's foremost political leaders: "He treats knowledge as if it were dangerous to his convictions. Often it is."[7] Such is the appeal of a cherished ideology that we are prone to accept only evidence that seems to support it and discard what does not.

We also have reason to beware of people who claim a direct line from God on public policy issues, who oversimplify, underanalyze, and are contemptuous of those who differ with them. In the carrying out of responsible citizenship there are plenty of reasons for humility, none for arrogance. Overweening certainty on political agendas masks insecurity and ignorance. So we do well to distinguish between the confidence of faith, to which we are urged, and the fleshly yearning for security—that comfortable feeling of mastery over matters about which God has not yet tipped his hand.

At the outset of this chapter I noted that we are all prone to be captives of our surrounding culture. All of us live under the temptation of letting our faith and ethical principles serve secular values to which we pledge our real allegiance. Doing so is a form of idolatry, a way of being "conformed to this world" (Rom. 12:2, RSV). The radical call of Jesus is that instead of being conformed to the world, we become transformed through him. Transformation in Christ brings with it a new relationship to everyone and everything—including, let us hope, public policies that deeply affect the lives of others. We have no divine prescriptions for public policy, no shortcuts to policy analysis. But we do have principles of faith, and these—not alien values—are to inform and guide us.

Transformation in Christ also means submitting our cherished policy opinions to God for change, recognizing that the more our opinions represent personal advantage to us (whether in terms of money, power, convenience, self-esteem, or approval

7. Broder, article opposite the editorial page in the *Washington Post,* 31 Dec. 1986.

from others), the more prone we are to self-deception concerning them, and the more we may implore God to sanction our opinions. Instead, we should pray for understandings that more nearly reflect God's will, and for the courage to act upon them.

Chapter 5
The Role of the Church

Isn't it strange that God has given you directly the answer—while he's given me the assignment?
> —Abraham Lincoln to clergymen who told him how to prosecute the war

The idea that moral sensitivity somehow bestows competence to make policy recommendations on every subject is delusional.
> —Peter L. Berger

Many of the most important modern insights about politics have come from the pens of theologians.
> —Hans J. Morgenthau, *Dilemmas of Politics*

In June 1982, a committee of Roman Catholic bishops, working on behalf of the National Conference of Catholic Bishops, released the first draft of an extensive report on the nuclear arms race. The report analyzed the main aspects of this issue, which it assessed in the light of Christian moral principles. The report immediately hit the front pages of newspapers, got coverage on television networks, and became the cover story of *Time, Newsweek,* and other magazines. Such media attention for a church's assessment of a public policy issue was unprecedented. Coming at a time when the "new religious right" had emerged as a major participant in the national political arena, the report underscored the involvement of churches in public affairs. In combination, these developments raised an important question to a new level of visibility: What is the proper role of the churches with regard to the affairs of government?

A Glance at History

Historically there have been various ways in which the church has related to the state and to matters of public policy. During the first three centuries A.D., the church in the Roman Empire grew as an outside religious sect. Oftentimes it was barely tolerated, and its members lived under a cloud of suspicion and were sometimes viciously persecuted. Under these circumstances, the church had little opportunity to influence public policy.

After Constantine became emperor in the early fourth century, the church began to receive more favorable treatment. Before the turn of the century, the church was fully established as an officially endorsed religious institution, with Christianity the favored religion of the Empire. The meaning of "favored religion" varied according to place and time within the Empire, and of course could not define the church's role at all in other parts of the world. This relationship between church and state offered advantages to both, but it also led to conflict, because the two did not always agree. Who was to make decisions when each claimed special interest or superior authority? Each had recognized functions that were respected by the other. But the church and the state also vied for control, each at times trying to extend its influence over the other or use the other for its own purposes, and each seeking to protect its own domain. The tensions of this relationship were evident in the practice of the pope crowning the emperor. This practice began with Charlemagne in the year 800 and ended in 1804, when Napoleon Bonaparte brought the pope to Paris for the coronation. During that ceremony Napoleon seized the crown from the pope and put it on his head himself.

This precarious relationship was affected by the Reformation, which brought about the breakup of the Holy Roman Empire. The result was a patchwork of states and principalities, each with its own preferred church. These arrangements were frequently challenged and sometimes led to brutal wars. The religious situation differed greatly from place to place, but the common pattern was one in which a state recognized Roman Catholicism or some form of Protestantism and discouraged or forbade dissent.

In North America the thirteen colonies became an experiment not only in democracy but also in religious pluralism. However, religious liberty came gradually. Even though many colonists had migrated to our shores in order to escape religious persecution, they usually sought to establish their own church as the recognized and dominant one. The Virginia colony and, later, other southern colonies made the Church of England the established church (that is, the church officially recognized and supported by the state). The Puritans in Massachusetts established what became the Congregational Church. The Dutch established the Reformed Church in New Amsterdam; it held sway until the British captured the colony, renamed it New York, and established the Church of England there. In fact, all but four of the thirteen colonies established one church or another as their official church. Some colonies actively persecuted dissenters. For example, the Massachusetts Puritans banished Roger Williams, one of their own ministers who became a Baptist, for criticizing such practices as civil punishment for those who broke the laws of the Sabbath. These Puritans not only banished Quakers, but decreed the death penalty for those who returned after banishment. In the South, Baptists were persecuted by state authorities.

Separation of Church and State

At the time of the Revolutionary War, nine of the thirteen colonies had "established" churches, and it was not until 1785 that one of them—the state of Virginia—enacted into law full religious liberty. It took almost another fifty years for the rest of the states to follow suit (Massachusetts was the last to do so). Meanwhile, the First Amendment to the Constitution outlawed religious establishment at the national level with these words: *"Congress shall make no law respecting an establishment of religion, or prohibiting the free exercise thereof."*

It should be noted that the Constitution does not use the phrase "separation of church and state," though that principle has been used by the U.S. Supreme Court and widely accepted as an application of the First Amendment's meaning. We have institutional separation but also functional interaction between church and state. The state has remained neutral with regard to the various religious institutions, but not neutral regarding religion. On the contrary, our government has positively encouraged the "free exercise" of religion. For example, churches are not required to pay taxes on property used for religious and charitable purposes. If a church building catches fire, the local fire department rushes to put out the blaze; the principle of separation is not invoked to prevent such assistance. School lunches, government loans to college students, the GI bill, and government research grants may benefit those attending or teaching at church-related institutions, because such benefits are seen as being provided to individuals on a fair and equal basis, not as favoring one religious group over another. The taxpayers of this country pay military chaplains to carry out a pastoral ministry among service personnel. Both the House and the Senate of the United States have a chaplain who opens the day's session with prayer. The list of interactions goes on and on—and so do matters of concern. Each year the U.S. Supreme Court is asked to rule on cases that raise new questions and call for further clarification in determining what is an appropriate functional relationship between church and state and what crosses over the line separating the two institutions.

We need to do more than find out what is constitutionally permissible, however. We should also consider what is advisable. That point has been raised by many Christians, including members of Congress, regarding such issues as spoken prayer in public schools. If we make such prayer inoffensive, are we inviting a bland, nondescript, general prayer that is devoid of all particularity (say, reference to Jesus as Lord and Savior) and therefore unacceptable to some? If we make the prayer more particular, will it be offensive to others? Or consider the practice of having clergy offer prayers and benedictions at political conventions or campaign rallies. This strikes me as a manipulation of religion to serve political ends, often highly partisan political ends, and to relegate religion to a safely decorative role. God is praised, thanked, and invoked for all manner of candidates and causes. It seems to me that it is much better if the church deals head-on with specific issues that it feels morally compelled and equipped to address.

These concerns are part of a much wider question: When is the church fulfilling its unique and distinctive mission as the church, and when is it presenting a blurred vision? When is it being co-opted by the state for purposes that may be alien to the church? There are no easy answers to these questions, because the answers need to be given on a case-by-case basis, in response to countless specific situations, and Christians often will not assess these situations in the same way.

Religion and Life: No Grounds for Divorce

I want to stress again the importance of distinguishing between the separation of church and state, and the separation of religion and life. The latter puts much of life outside the boundary of faith, contradicting the reality that Jesus Christ is Lord of our entire life. The distinction applies to the church as well as to the individual, though one often hears clergy and laity alike suggest that the church has no business dealing with policy issues.

"The church's job is to preach the gospel, not get involved in politics," it is said—and there is a sense in which this pronouncement is valid. It is a mistake for churches to get mired in *partisan* politics. It is the essence of the church's mission and ministry to preach, teach, and celebrate God's work of redeeming us through Jesus Christ. However, such preaching and celebration cannot occur in a vacuum. They occur in the context of real life and real problems, both individual and social. Thus proclaiming and celebrating the gospel faithfully means doing so specifically—for example, in relation to the family. Not the family as an abstraction, but the real family that one belongs to—your family or my family—composed of people with warts, wrinkles, and clay feet, with joys and heartaches, growing pains and needs. Through our families God has placed most of us in a position of special responsibility toward some very precious people. Because our understanding and our capacity to respond are limited, we need to do all that we can to help one another strengthen our family relationships so that our hopes for one another and the steps we take to realize these hopes partake more fully of God's intention for us. If someone were to tell us that it is the church's job to preach the gospel and not to get involved in family life, we would instinctively protest that the church, if it is to proclaim and live the gospel faithfully, must necessarily be involved in matters of family life and cannot possibly remove so important an area of life from its concern. If Jesus has no place in my family concerns, then he is not truly my Lord and Savior.

For much the same reason, the church cannot duck public issues of exceptional importance that profoundly affect the lives of others. That leaves open the question of *how* it should respond. There are wise ways and foolish ways, of course. But the church does not faithfully respond to the biblical witness regarding the injustice of hunger, for example, unless it pays attention to policy decisions that affect the hungry. More broadly cast, the church should not use the need to distance itself from partisan politics as an excuse to avoid speaking out on political issues of great moral importance.

Let me be clear. The church relates to society primarily through the conversion of people and their nurture in faith. Changed lives make a lasting impact on society, and this is by far the most important way in which the church contributes to the wholeness of the world. My thinking is in harmony with this reality, not in competition with it. Service to Christ through citizenship falls within the mission of the church to help people grow in discipleship. But if people are brought to Christ and nourished in Christ by a congregation that avoids engagement with public policy matters, these Christians are being led to believe that a vast arena of life, though it vitally affects the well-being of others, is of no particular concern to God. The love and lordship of Christ are viewed in a way that fails to encompass the whole of life. By choosing "not to get involved" in public policy issues, a congregation shortchanges its members regarding their ministry and stewardship.

In reality there is no such thing as "not getting involved" or never taking a stand on critical moral issues, because not taking a stand *is* taking a stand in support of the status quo or the direction in which things may be moving. The classic example of this is provided by the church in Germany during the rise of Hitler. There were notable and courageous exceptions, to be sure, but for the most part, pastors, priests, and laypeople said the church should stick to preaching the gospel and stay away from politics. It was a comfortable, safe response. But in retrospect it is clear that far from being uninvolved in politics, the church was deeply mired in it, for the church's neutrality was understood as consent to the Nazi program. The church's neutrality was an illusion, a tragic misjudgment.

Local Churches and Policy Issues

When we ask how a local church can best address public policy issues, the answer first of all is that the church's essential task is not that of addressing public policy issues but the ministry of the gospel or, put differently, the carrying out of the Great Commission of Jesus. That said, it must immediately be added that this ministry of the gospel, this commission to make disciples, has as a major purpose the calling and equipping of people in Christ for a life of service. It is in this connection that the local church should see its public policy role. How can its members be equipped for service to others? That service, if fully embraced, includes the offering of our citizenship to God for the benefit of others, and part of Christian citizenship is the advocating of policies that will enhance human life.

The local church can do this in ways that the national church body cannot, because the local church is where the people are. Quintessentially, the church is the local communion of believers, not a national institution. It is here that God's people gather to pray, praise, and nourish one another in the life of faith. And so here, most of all, is where the opportunity lies for integrating public policy concerns into a full expression of the gospel. Either that happens in the local congregation, or it probably does not happen at all.

The Sunday worship (service, mass) is only the first and most important of ways in which a local church can develop its commitment and understanding with regard to Christ and the world. The development of such commitment will embrace much more than public policy issues. These should be seen in the larger context of citizenship and the still larger context of one's whole life as an offering to God. Participating in the local PTA, serving on the local school board, taking part in a neighborhood improvement campaign, or becoming active in the local precinct of one's political party—these are among the many ways in which people can get involved, for good reasons or bad, in public affairs. Christians should be encouraged to think about such involvement as a specifically Christian ministry and given opportunity to discuss such service with fellow believers. This can be done in a way that does not divide people but helps them understand their Christian calling. Such a context provides a training ground and preparation for work on policy issues as well.

The role of church leaders, especially that of the pastor, deserves special comment. In my view, the pastor should not see himself or herself as a policy expert commissioned to deliver answers from the pulpit—a top-down approach that is inappropriate and seldom effective, as well as unfair to both the pastor and the congregation. This approach is apt to be divisive because people will see themselves pressed to embrace the pastor's political preferences, which, they may suspect, do not spring from divine revelation. A dose of well-founded humility on these matters will be greatly appreciated. What the faithful need in a pastor is a person who invites them to use their considerable gifts and insights in service to Christ, and who honestly struggles with them on some key issues. "When it comes to public policy," says Father Martin Hernardy of St. Stephen's parish in Toledo, Ohio, "we are all Indians. There are no chiefs." A slight exaggeration, but he makes a point. Asking the right questions, providing opportunities and resources for people to consider them, and nurturing potential leaders works better than handing out solutions. Such an approach nourishes others because it respects their experience and lodges trust in them as people of God who can be counted on to respond to the lordship of Jesus in the public policy arena. This is the kind of challenge that some people can get excited about.

The pastor and other leaders in the local church do well to guard against moralism. By moralism I mean exhortations to do good ("Write your member of Congress about the famine in Africa") that are not grounded in God's saving love and therefore do not sound like an opportunity to love and serve God in return. The desired action should be presented as an invitation to respond to the gospel and human need. The word "invitation" is crucial, because the intention should not be to pressure people into an action or to make them feel like moral lepers if they do not respond in a certain way, but to let them experience the joy of serving others.

In addition, it is unfair to ask people to take actions for which they do not feel sufficiently prepared. Not everyone is at the same level of preparation or can be expected to arrive at the same conclusion regarding the best course of action. So it is wise if, within the context of a grace-oriented invitation (as opposed to a law-oriented exhortation), the pastor gives members of the congregation the time and opportunity to consider an issue together.

The Sunday worship (service, mass) is the heart of the congregation's life as a community of believers, so what happens here affects everything else. The biblical lessons or texts used in most churches provide a wide range of opportunities—too seldom utilized—to bring various issues to the congregation's attention. The preaching, the prayers, and even the singing can and should reflect a ministry to the world—but not in a way that makes people feel badgered and certainly not in a way that detracts from the centrality of God's love in Christ. Attention to our earthly citizenship should not make us feel that our heavenly citizenship is being slighted. The latter reality should, in fact, inform and motivate us regarding the former.

The typical congregation also has other tools that can be utilized to encourage service through citizenship. Even a minute or two of thought produces a list of possibilities, including the church bulletin, a newsletter, Sunday school, Bible class, auxiliary organizations, church committees, the church council, annual planning meetings that establish goals, church dinners, special events, youth activities, pastoral visits, and neighborhood cluster groups. Much that is constructive can take place informally in discussions after church, around the edges of meetings, in homes, at church picnics, and the like. The list will vary from church to church, but opportunities abound.

Planning is crucial. Important goals are seldom reached by chance, and if ways of dealing with policy issues are not in some manner built into the life of the parish through deliberate planning, they are unlikely to get serious attention, and one important aspect of Christian service will go largely unconsidered. At Bread for the World this need was called to our attention so often by pastors and lay leaders that we finally designed a Covenant Church Program to respond to it. The basic idea is to provide a way in which a congregation can make hunger an ongoing concern in its life. This doesn't happen automatically; it has to be planned. Initially it may come as a suggestion from the pastor or a lay member or, preferably, a small nucleus of committed individuals. The pastor needs to be involved and usually so does a social concerns committee or the church council. The key step is to get a few people to sit down together and determine some reasonable, achievable goals. Perhaps the group could choose just one goal to start with, and once that has been accomplished, it could choose a few more for a six-month or twelve-month period.

A key question for local church leaders to ask is, How can Christians best equip themselves for ministry as citizen advocates? Regardless of what steps are taken in response to that question, the initiators should anticipate reluctance. People are busy. They feel unprepared and fearful. The idea of writing a letter to someone in government may intimidate them. They may not be entirely convinced that public policy is a legitimate arena for Christian service. And, after all, most of us take a long time to change our habits and attitudes. Groundwork needs to be laid, and gains usually come slowly. God has not said that every Christian must be a citizen advocate, and we should not say so, either. At the same time, Christians can be helped to see a vastly neglected opportunity for service. Some can be persuaded to serve as citizen advocates if they see such service as directly and importantly related to the well-being of others, and therefore a way of celebrating the gospel.

An advocate is one who pleads the cause of another. So the work of citizen advocacy should not be entirely foreign to Christians. After all, we have an advocate in the Father (1 John 2:1), and it is he who calls us to care about others and speak up on their behalf.

National Church Bodies and Policy Issues

There is widespread wariness in local congregations about the role of national church bodies in relation to public policy issues. One reason for such wariness is the feeling of many that "the church should stick to religion"—a feeling that is at least partly misguided. Another reason is that church members who express their views are sometimes challenged, and that seldom induces comfort. Those challenged often feel that their views have not been taken into account by leaders who have imposed their own flawed conclusions. This feeling is also partly misguided because there are often sound theological reasons for challenging views in the pews. All of this said, the uneasiness regarding the role of national church bodies in relation to policy issues, as well as the response to that uneasiness, should be considered from this standpoint: that the ministry of the church, including its ministry in the public policy arena, belongs to all of the people of God.

Church leaders have a special opportunity to guide the church in addressing policy issues; they should bear in mind that their task is ultimately to help equip Christians in the local congregations for effective service. However, church members do not have to wait passively for others in the church to speak for them. The principle that applies in government applies in the church as well: Those willing to take part in considering an issue and expressing views on it will have an influence far greater than their numbers simply because most other people do not bother to get involved in policy issues.

Selection of Issues. Since church bodies cannot address every policy issue that comes along, the selection of issues is important. As a rule, the fewer issues they address, the more they may be able to focus well and effectively. Questions like those following might serve as guidelines for selecting issues:

1. Which issues facing the nation could, in the light of biblical witness, be considered matters of critical moral concern (in contrast to those that are interesting or may be getting media exposure but are of comparatively less consequence)?

2. How many people are affected by a given issue, and how seriously are they affected?

3. What special contribution could a church body make with regard to a particular issue?

4. Is the issue one that is exceptionally important for Christians in local congregations to consider and do something about?

5. Can the issue be addressed in a way that gets at causes as well as symptoms?

Official Statements. One of the most common ways in which national church bodies address public policy issues is through official statements. These may be issued by a council of bishops, a church commission, or a group of delegates at a national church convention. They may come from a wider national or international body of Christians representing one or many denominations. Or they may come from a single authority, such as the pope, who from time to time writes encyclicals (letters to the church) on social and moral issues.

Issuing statements is one thing. Getting people to consider and act on them is quite another. With notable exceptions, official statements are widely ignored. They may still have considerable importance, perhaps influencing people at various levels of leadership, but usually they do not get attention within local congregations because such statements are seldom discussed there. If this is true of the response of local churches to statements from national church bodies, it is even more true of the response of Protestants to reports or resolutions coming from associations that represent many church bodies or from a worldwide denominational gathering. My impression is that Christians in local churches tend to think that their own denominational leadership is none too close to them, and that the larger national and international entities to which their denomination belongs are still further removed, so they do not readily identify with these groups. In addition, if my sense of the situation is correct, most church members are not all that interested in public policy issues, and many who are tend to think that church groups and church leaders possess no better understanding of such issues than they do. Whatever the reasons, official church statements are not automatic attention-getters.

What is the "target group" for such statements? The general public may sometimes be perceived as the audience, but it pays little attention—though there are exceptions to this rule. Even if statements occasionally get media coverage, they are quickly forgotten by most of the public. Are public officials the intended audience? Members of Congress seldom hold their breath waiting to see what the Presbyterians or the Baptists or any other denomination has to say about an issue, although there may be scattered interest. No, the people for whom such statements are primarily intended are the members of the religious body that issues the statements. *The key question, therefore, is how effectively does a statement invite members of local churches to think about an issue, discuss it, and take subsequent action?* And if the action is to influence a policy decision, then we are back to the basic matters of citizenship and advocacy.

What determines whether a policy statement is taken seri-

ously and has substantial influence, or is overwhelmingly ignored? Let me suggest three factors:

1. *The nature of the issue.* The issue itself has to be one that
people readily perceive as highly significant. If it is not so perceived, count on an uphill struggle.

2. *The quality of work done on the issue.* By "the quality of
work" I mean the development of a sound theological and moral
base as well as careful policy analysis. Regarding the latter, the
church has no particular shortcuts or revelations to substitute
for good analysis, and to the extent that good intentions are
offered instead (a frequent occurrence), statements tend to be
disregarded and may even do more harm than good.

3. *The extent to and manner in which congregational members
are invited to participate in considering an issue.* A well-chosen
issue and careful analysis do not guarantee effectiveness. Even
with careful policy analysis, the church usually does better offering directions than directives. Most Christians who are interested in policy issues are not prone to accept top-down
pronouncements uncritically. Such pronouncements do not sufficiently respect what they may have to contribute to the discussion and seldom motivate them to thought and action. As a
rule, the best time to involve people at the parish level is *during*
the development of a statement.

The Catholic bishops' pastoral on the nuclear arms race is an
instructive example, because it apparently made a strong impact
on Catholic thinking. The Reverend Andrew M. Greeley of the
National Opinion Research Center points out that before the
report was issued, 32 percent of U.S. Catholics thought that too
much money was being spent on armaments and defense—precisely the same percentage that held for Protestants. A year after
the report was issued, 32 percent still held for Protestants, but
the number of Catholics opposed to the amount of defense
spending had jumped to 54 percent. This figure reflected "an
astonishing social change in so short a time," according to Greeley, who added, "It is difficult to think of what other factor
beside the letter could affect Catholics and not Protestants in
this country."[1] I am aware of no other instance in which a re-

1. Greeley, "Who Leads Catholics?" *New York Times,* 8 Mar. 1985.

ligious statement on a public policy issue has brought about such a change.

Why? What accounts for this change? Some Protestants might suppose that it is the hierarchy at work: When the bishops speak, Catholics fall in line. But this is not the case; this has seldom happened, at least in recent history, on other issues. One example, as Greeley noted, are the repeated statements issued by the pope and bishops regarding sexual morality and birth control; these have not shifted Catholic opinion, which has moved slightly away from the views being urged by the hierarchy on those issues. So the explanation lies elsewhere. Though I can't prove it, I believe that the explanation is largely related to the three factors just listed.

First, the issue was perceived by the general public, including Catholics, as one of exceptional significance. An unusual surge of interest surrounded this issue prior to the bishops' report, so the national media were quick to feature the pastoral. This interest and coverage gave the report an extraordinary advantage.

Second, whether or not the bishops came to the right conclusions, their analytical work was exceptionally thorough. An unusual amount of time was invested by well-qualified staff members to develop drafts of this book-length proposal. The committee of bishops that produced these drafts held numerous hearings at which they received testimony and engaged in discussion with dozens of experts who represented various sides of the issue. These included former secretaries of state and former secretaries of defense as well as high-level Administration officials. The moral and the technical arguments were carefully developed. Seldom in U.S. history has the position of a national church body on a public policy issue been so painstakingly researched and composed.

Third, the bishops were astute in casting the document not as the last word on the subject—an edict from the authorities— but as an invitation to Catholics in every parish across the land to discuss the issue of nuclear arms. To accent participation, the bishops published a preliminary draft of the work to invite suggestions. This was deft strategy: it not only resulted in a better report but assured more parishioner involvement. Even though a small percentage of Catholics participated in discussions at the parish level, parishioners were aware of the opportunity for participation and the fact that the discussions occurred, and this helped evoke confidence. Had the same report been issued as a top-down pronouncement, it probably would have had more limited influence. But as an invitation to reflection and response, it worked well.

In addition, the bishops distinguished between moral principles, which they drew from the Catholic Christian tradition, and recommendations based on policy analysis. They acknowledged that the latter did not carry the same level of authority, and pointed out that Catholics could disagree with them in good conscience. This acknowledgment added credibility to the report and encouraged open discussion.

Having cited this example, I need to add a qualification. In November 1984 the U.S. Catholic bishops issued the preliminary draft of another lengthy report, this one on the U.S. economy, following the same general process they had used to generate the earlier report. Subsequently, a national survey found a wide gap of opinion between Catholic priests and lay people on the question of whether or not "bishops should take public stands on some political issues such as the arms race or the American economic system." Eighty percent of the priests said that they should do so, while only 39 percent of the lay people approved of such action.[2] Even if one allows that the adjective "political" (instead of, say, "moral") might have invited a negative response, the survey suggests that Catholic laity may not feel as well consulted and drawn into the process as I have supposed. Whatever the reasons for the response of the laity in this instance, the survey underscores the importance of lay participation.

There is no perfect process that ought always to be followed in developing official statements, but church members need to be drawn into the process, for their ministry, their Christian service, is paramount. The process will vary because circumstances and issues as well as church bodies are so varied. During the 1950s and 1960s, for example, most denominations took a stand on civil rights and on the nature of the church as inclusive

2. See Dean R. Hoge, Joseph J. Shields, and Mary Jeanne Verdieck, "Attitudes of Priests, Adults, and College Students on Catholic Parish Life and Leadership," Catholic University of America, 1986. Photocopy.

of all races. A majority of congregations did not discuss these emerging positions, and no doubt more should have been done to encourage such discussion. Nevertheless, certain events, theological integrity, and the leadership of some congregations and individuals combined to prompt national church bodies to speak an official word. Both before and after positions were articulated, a sometimes painfully slow galvanizing of opinion occurred, a process in which the development of church statements was useful. In my own church body, the Lutheran Human Relations Association played a key role in this process by informing congregations and prodding church leadership. Other groups played a similar role in other church bodies. In the end the impact both on the churches and on the nation was considerable.

I am giving more attention to the question of official statements than to other ways in which national church bodies take up public policy issues. This is misleading in a way, but I choose this emphasis because I think there is confusion regarding the purpose of such statements, a tendency to think of them as ends in themselves rather than as means of engaging Christians in ministry.

Washington Offices. Most large denominations have a Washington office on public affairs; sometimes a number of denominations are represented by one office. These offices serve several purposes. They are listening posts for the church bodies they represent. They inform the leadership and membership regarding issues that are perceived to be of special importance to these bodies. And they will occasionally take positions consistent with the policy of these bodies and lobby for these positions by meeting with government officials or presenting testimony to congressional committees.

Church Staff. Most religious bodies also have departments that seek to get church members to consider various issues. They prepare and publish study materials and organize conferences for this purpose. Most denominations carry out this function through a department of social ministries or a department of church and society. The Christian Life Commission serves in this way for the Southern Baptist Convention, for example. Roman Catholics have an office on justice and peace in each diocese.

Often more important is what happens outside these designated channels, as the following questions suggest:

- What kinds of articles are featured in church publications?
- What is offered to adults and children through parish education materials?
- What do church leaders talk about when they address their clergy and lay people?

In each of these areas, members of any congregation can help decide what happens by writing or talking to those in charge. They may submit an article, for example, offer to develop a Sunday school course if they have that ability, or invite a church leader to speak on a particular issue.

The role of the church in relation to public policy is multi-faceted. In considering that role, I want to focus on these questions: How effectively are parishioners being engaged in thought and action? Is their ministry being neglected? Or are they being invited to participate as Christians and as citizens in service to others?

Chapter 6
Public Policy Groups

> In any open contest, unless there are compensating factors, the less ambiguous vision, though false, will be more immediately attractive than the one that demands patience or allows for doubt and "on the other hands." It will also be more likely to have been found dangerous or wrong tomorrow.
> —Martin E. Marty, *The Public Church*

> Just as politics can become an idol, so religion can become an idol. . . . Today we witness a strange convergence of idolatrous propensities. . . . It happens when political goals are incorporated within and equated with what Christianity means by salvation. It matters little whether the political goal be liberation through class struggle or the victory of freedom through the defeat of Communism.
> —Richard John Neuhaus, *The Naked Public Square*

> Certainly we do not want men to allow their Christianity to flow over into their political life, for the establishment of anything like a really just society would be a major disaster. On the other hand we do want, and want very much, to make men treat Christianity as a means; preferably, of course, as a means to their own advancement, but, failing that, as a means to anything—even to social justice.
> —the devil Screwtape in *The Screwtape Letters* by C. S. Lewis

In order to serve Christ and others in the arena of government policy, Christians can join public interest groups that specialize in one or several issues. None of us can work in isolation and expect to accomplish much. We ordinarily need to work with others to exert influence for policy change. In our political system, group action is by far the most effective way to move government, and public policy groups provide an avenue for such action.

Let me put it another way. Private lobbyists fulfill an important function by furnishing legislators and government officials with vital information on matters about which they need to cast votes or make administrative decisions. But if we do not want to leave such influential activity entirely in the hands of special interests that have their own advantage—often financial—to promote, then we must make our opinions known to the decision-makers. By doing so we act as *citizen* lobbyists or advocates. Ordinarily we do this most effectively if we follow the advice of a group that specializes in an issue. Organized action is effective because it is planned and coordinated, while the isolated efforts of individuals tend to be scattered and poorly timed.

Before joining any policy group, of course, it makes sense to examine its stance carefully and compare its views with competing views on the same issue or issues.

Options for Involvement

Could the church assume the function of public interest groups for Christians? The social justice networks cited in the last chapter illustrate one way in which some religious denominations do this on a small scale. However, national church bodies and local churches can't take a stand on every important policy issue, let alone each related piece of legislation. They have neither the staff nor the expertise to do so, and in any case, doing so would require an inappropriately large amount of time, energy, and resources. Yet it is important for Christians to consider issues from a faith perspective and make their opinions known to lawmakers when decisions are pending. One way that denominations and local churches foster responsible citizenship on the part of their members is by encouraging participation in public interest groups. As a result, more Christians become citizen advocates. But the church as such is not expected to make countless policy judgments.

Regarding the issue of hunger, for example, the stated views of national church bodies reflect extensive agreement on underlying principles and the direction in which those principles should carry us. But the issue of hunger involves many specific and often highly technical pieces of legislation each year. A few denominations have developed small networks of people at the local level to take action on these, but no single denomination has the staff to do extensive policy analysis on such legislation, prepare and disseminate material on it, keep track of it as it moves through various levels of Congress, and propose and negotiate the introduction of new legislation. Consequently, most national church bodies support Bread for the World, draw on our policy analysis, and encourage membership in Bread for the World. Because our organization is explicitly Christian yet politically nonpartisan, national church bodies have felt comfortable with it. Its independence spares them the onus of having to defend each position of Bread for the World as representing their own official stand.

Bread for the World is not the only church-related policy group working on the hunger issue, although it is the only one working exclusively on hunger. Interfaith Action for Economic Justice—an instrument of a number of religious bodies, most of which belong to the National Council of Churches (NCC)—deals with hunger along with other economic issues. Indirectly it has a membership network by virtue of its relationship with IMPACT, a citizen-lobbyist arm of the Washington Interreligious Staff Council (an association built around a core of NCC-related offices on public affairs). Network and the Friends Committee on National Legislation are two other citizens' lobbies that deal with a wide range of issues that sometimes includes hunger.

In addition to the groups mentioned above, numerous national and local church-related groups work on issues such as abortion, disarmament, and prison reform. Some groups deal with only one issue, some with more than one. The approaches they take and the quality of their work vary considerably, so it is important to review them carefully before joining them. But they do offer Christians an opportunity to become active in public affairs.

Not all policy groups are primarily lobbying organizations. Some specialize in policy analysis or education. For example, the Association for Public Justice is attempting to develop a nonpartisan understanding of public policy consistent with an evangelical theology. It also presents occasional testimony before Congress. This association functions as a small think tank, as do the Center of Concern, which is a Roman Catholic organization; the Center for Theology and Public Policy, which is attached to Wesley Theological Seminary (based in Washington, D.C.); and the Center on Religion and Society (based in New York). All of these groups are based in Washington. Each in its own way is plowing new ground.

Most public policy groups are not church-related, and most do not deal primarily, if at all, with hunger. The League of Women Voters, for example, has a wide-ranging policy agenda that occasionally includes issues related to hunger. Like most public interest groups, the League draws many Christians into its membership. Whether their focus is on one or several issues, these groups offer both Christians and non-Christians an opportunity to work on policies that have an important bearing on the well-being of others and on society as a whole.

What I have done here is simply outline what a few policy organizations do, giving just a hint of the enormous variety of organizations, some related to the church and some not, through which Christians can serve.

The Flaws of the New Religious Right

Among church-related policy groups, the Liberty Federation (formerly the Moral Majority) is by far the largest and, some observers would argue, the most influential. The Liberty Federation is a project of and the leading voice of what is called "the new religious right." Though technically not Christian, the Liberty Federation counts among its members many supporters of nationally prominent TV evangelists, especially the Reverend Jerry Falwell, who is the Federation president. The Federation is aggressively patriotic in its appeal to return this country to traditional moral values. There is much to be said for patriotism and traditional moral values. Unfortunately, the Liberty Federation and associated groups such as the Christian Voice, the Roundtable, and the American Coalition for Traditional Values appear to be captive to a right-wing ideology and press their beliefs into its service. Christians captive to a left-wing ideology would deserve equal criticism, but there is no comparable religiously oriented left-wing policy group or movement in the United States. I comment on the new religious right because it has skyrocketed to public importance, and as a faith-motivated movement it prompts frequent questions concerning Christian citizenship and the relationship of faith to public policy.

Among the contributions of the Liberty Federation, the Christian Voice, and related groups is their success in persuading millions of Christians across the land that it is not only permissible but imperative for Christians to take action in the policy arena. That in itself is an astounding accomplishment. In addition, they have highlighted the danger of moral decay and encouraged people not simply to deplore it but to do something about it. These strengths notwithstanding, the new religious right is gravely flawed on the following counts:

1. *Its issue agenda.* Some of its concerns—such as the federal deficit, abortion, and family instability—certainly have a place among the policy considerations of Christians. But the overall agenda of the new religious right has a negative cast characterized by frequent opposition to positions that have obtained fairly broad bipartisan support and that seem consistent, on the surface at least, with biblical exhortations regarding justice and peace. For example, the new religious right has opposed the following:

- a U.S. department of education
- a treaty with Panama returning eventual control of the canal to that country
- federal funding for programs to assist battered wives
- minimum wage laws
- food stamps
- U.S. recognition of the People's Republic of China
- the Equal Rights Amendment

I am not suggesting that each of the above measures self-evidently merits the support of Christians, or that each offers the most promising way to achieve its stated goals. However, given the intent of each and the extent of bipartisan backing for each, the burden of proof lies with those who maintain that Christians are morally obligated to rise up and oppose these measures.

Even more puzzling than what is included in the agenda of the new religious right is what has been excluded. Where are the issues of hunger and poverty, or the issue of basic justice for the oppressed, about which the Bible has a great deal more to say than it does about canal treaties?

One is left to conclude that such an agenda has been shaped by extreme political views, not a biblical mandate.

2. *Its analysis.* The new religious right's analysis of issues is regrettably shallow. Its analysis is no less shallow for claiming to be based on biblical principles. *Christianity Today,* regarded by many as the leading journal for conservative evangelicals, had this to say in a feature-length editorial: "How can a policy board of evangelical Christians, without access to vast amounts of intricate political data, emerge from a meeting and announce that it has arrived at the Christian or moral position on lifting sanctions against Zimbabwe [then white-controlled Rhodesia], for example?"[1]

3. *Its direct movement from the Bible to policy positions.* In Liberty Federation pronouncements there has been no admission of difficulty in determining God's will for the nation on specific issues, no hint of struggle or uncertainty on these matters, only absolute assurance that one can move from faith to policy prescription, even on positions that are implausible on specifically Christian grounds. For years Falwell attacked the 1954 U.S. Supreme Court decision against segregation in the public schools and, later, the civil rights legislation of the 1960s (all plots hatched in Moscow, he said) on the grounds that the Bible supported separation of the races. Fortunately, he has reversed his position on these issues. But now he arrives with equal certainty at other positions that seem no less artificially related to the Bible.

4. *Its judgmental stance.* Given our human limitations, a certain amount of modesty and tolerance rings true in the public policy arena. But those who take positions that differ from those of the new religious right have frequently been denounced, accused of undermining the nation's moral foundations. In addition, their positions have sometimes been misrepresented. For example, the Christian Voice has listed a vote to fund centers for battered wives as an anti-family vote, and a vote against preventing the IRS from denying tax-exempt status to private schools

1. "Getting God's Kingdom into Politics," *Christianity Today,* 19 Sept. 1980, p. 11.

that racially discriminate as a vote against protecting Christian schools.[2]

This judgmental stance led Senator Barry Goldwater (R-Ariz.), whose credentials as a conservative few would challenge, to issue a major public statement assailing the Liberty Federation (then the Moral Majority) and other groups associated with the new religious right. "I can say with conviction that the religious issues of these groups have little or nothing to do with conservative or liberal politics," said Goldwater. He called their uncompromising position "a divisive element that could tear apart the very spirit of our representative system, if they gain sufficient strength." And he added some advice: "They must learn to make their views known without trying to make their views the only alternatives."[3]

A more recent comment comes from U.S. Secretary of Education William J. Bennett in a speech he delivered at the University of Missouri in September 1986: "On the one hand, religion should never be excluded from public debate. But on the other, it should never be used as a kind of divine trump card to foreclose further debate. Those who claim that their religious faith gives them a monopoly on political truth make democratic discourse difficult."

All of us know the temptation to be judgmental, especially when we feel deeply about an issue and others disagree. I face that temptation and do not always emerge unscathed with regard to Bread for the World's hunger agenda. I believe that thousands and sometimes millions of lives are affected by the outcome of votes in Congress, and when I see a senator or representative consistently vote in a way that appears to be against people who are at high risk, it is agonizing. But Bread for the World does not accuse those who vote against its positions of taking unChristian or immoral stands. Years ago we issued "Loaves" and "Crumbs" ratings—the former to members of Congress who had a good voting record on our issues, the latter to members who had a zero voting record on those issues. We stopped that because it sounded excessively negative. We continue to issue

2. Paul Simon, *The Glass House: Politics and Morality in the Nation's Capital* (New York: Continuum, 1984), p. 90.

3. Goldwater, as quoted in the *New York Times*, 16 Sept. 1981, pp. 1, 89.

congressional report cards each year based on the voting records of each member of the House and Senate on hunger-related legislation, and we publicize these records. But we acknowledge that hunger is not the only issue on which people should judge those who serve in Congress, and we recognize that a legislator's work in committee or behind the scenes may be more important than his or her voting record.

Why is the new religious right so rigid, so certain, so prone to stand in judgment of those who disagree? My own view is that its certainty masks a profound insecurity, an insecurity that stems from an awful sense that our moral foundations are rapidly eroding, being washed away by an environment that is hostile to faith. Those who sense this erosion are not exactly mistaken, although I think they exaggerate its uniqueness for our moment in history. The increases in crime, drug abuse, divorce, and permissive sex, to name a few present-day scourges, are no mirage. Television entertainers and advertisers have become purveyors—new priests—of moral values who invade the privacy of our homes and the minds of our children. None of us escapes this influence. Whether we are willing victims or unwilling resisters, we are not left untouched. The adverse influence pervades our lives, affecting our churches, schools, homes, and neighborhoods. Is it any wonder, then, that millions of Christians feel deeply threatened? This insecurity gives rise to a great longing for solutions to these and other problems, such as the threat of Communism and the perceived decline in U.S. prestige abroad. As a result, many have seized a package of ready-made answers that promises to set the world in order again, a world that seems to be getting out of control. The possibility that these people may have put their finger on some critical problems or that they may even be on the right track on some issues seems inadmissible to the political left, which has ideological blinders and judgmental dispositions of its own. The new religious right illustrates that when Christians embrace a policy agenda that is captive to any ideology and that is promoted in the name of God, they play dangerously with the lives of others.

Time may bring moderation to the new religious right. The Moral Majority's changing its name in 1986 to the Liberty Federation was widely interpreted as an attempt to deal with an unusually high negative rating in public opinion polls. Perhaps the change will be more than one of name. Perhaps the Liberty Federation, along with other groups of the new religious right, will become less ideological and more open to justice for the oppressed. I hope so, because if that happens, hungry people (among others) will greatly benefit. If it does not happen, many Christians within the new religious right will become disenchanted and cynical or look for approaches to public policy that are more faithful to the Bible.

Cultural captivity is not unique to the new religious right. For example, to the extent that they embrace Marxism, some forms of liberation theology have likewise seized a system of ready-made answers for straightening out the social order and have pressed theology into their service. If the religious right is ideologically prone to support right-wing totalitarian governments on the grounds that they are anti-Communist, the religious left, which claims to be more concerned about human rights, tends to overlook the absence of such rights in Marxist-dominated countries. Many on the religious right have supported the discredited Somozan regime in Nicaragua and, more recently, the Contras, while many on the religious left have taken a see-no-evil view of the Sandinistas.

The religious left can be just as thoroughly seduced by ideological or cultural sirens, just as prone to leap from faith to policy positions, and just as judgmental as the religious right. Secular rather than Christian values can capture our allegiance whether our politics are right, left, or center. In truth, none of us completely escapes such captivity. In politics as in the rest of life, we are all more prone than we realize to be influenced by values alien to faith. All the more reason, then, to be "wise as serpents" in our pursuit of better public policies. All the more reason to acknowledge that we live by the grace of forgiveness.

The presence of public policy groups alerts us to several dangers that Christians face in the policy arena. One danger is that of becoming ideologically captive—a form of idolatry. Another danger is single-issue politics: judging candidates for public office only by their stand on a single issue, such as gun control, abortion, or even hunger. But on the positive side, public policy groups also offer Christians an opportunity to participate actively and responsibly in a ministry of service to others.

Chapter 7
Living with Limitations

> But we have this treasure in earthen vessels, to show that the
> transcendent power belongs to God and not to us.
>
> —Saint Paul, 2 Cor. 4:7

> Since nothing we intend is ever faultless, and nothing we
> attempt ever without error, and nothing we achieve without
> some measure of finitude and fallibility we call humanness,
> we are saved by forgiveness.
>
> —David Augsburger, Caring Enough to Forgive

> Forgive us our virtues,
> As we forgive those who are virtuous against us.
>
> —Chad Walsh

We can do a great deal for others in the policy arena if we are
willing to cope with the real world and its limitations rather
than fabricating an ideal world. An ideal world is much easier
to take on. In such a world we move from one victory to another,
success ever within our grasp. People respond to us the way we
want them to. The rightness of our cause is recognized, and our
work is appreciated by others. We seldom make mistakes, en-
tertain doubts, or become discouraged. It is a great world but,
alas, a world of our own imagination, and if we allow it to
establish the conditions for our participation in public policy
choices, we will become disillusioned.

The real world, like the work to which God calls us, is much
grubbier. It is full of obstacles, not the least of which are our
own shortcomings. In this world, victories are infrequent and
hard to come by, and we make gains only with difficulty. Hunger and injustice abound, struggle is assured, and success is
always in doubt. But this is the world in which God calls us to

make a difference. God has chosen to use earthen vessels for the task, not angels. And through us God is willing to work miracles, but not magic.

Let me candidly describe a few of the limitations we face.

Human Nature and Social Change

I believe that the future is with God and God's kingdom, and therefore I am an optimist. I also believe that human nature is instinctively selfish, and therefore the world is incurably resistant to anything like the advent of complete justice and peace. So we have to work for the best we can get. The world is easily made worse, but it is improved only with great difficulty. No matter how good we think our proposed solutions are, our best intentions and our best efforts are seriously flawed, and the kingdom of God stands in judgment of them all—which is not to say that all societies are equally flawed or that the degree to which they may reflect the vision of the kingdom (or its opposite) is of no consequence. It is of enormous consequence, just as the extent to which our individual lives reflect God's intention for us is of great consequence. This side of the Resurrection, a modest measure of justice may be the best we can hope to achieve, but working to achieve it represents a challenge of monumental importance. The elimination of hunger is, in my opinion, on the ambitious edge of a modest but attainable measure of justice.

Many Christians will view this opinion as much too optimistic. A friend of mine wrote to me, "I believe that the flaw that runs through human nature, original sin, runs through every aspect, including the intellect. With the best of intentions and political will and technical information we will still manage to mess things up. We shouldn't stop trying to do what we think best, but we should be prepared to see our best efforts produce unforeseen and unpalatable results." The point is a sobering one. Perhaps it means that ending hunger is beyond human reach. I allow for the possibility that I am wrong in viewing it as an attainable goal.

On the other hand, many of my co-believers of widely differing theological stances will consider my view to be excessively cautious and pessimistic. They speak of "social transformation."

I am not comfortable with that term because I think it promises too much. Of course it's possible to argue about what transformation means and define it in many different ways. The establishment and development of the United States was a social change of monumental importance. So was the elimination of slavery. So, for that matter, was the Russian revolution and its aftermath, though one would hardly propose that or the czarist regime that preceded it as a model. But "transformation" suggests to me a change for the better that is more sweeping than any we can reasonably expect in the kingdoms of this world. In the New Testament the word "transform" (literally the verb form of "metamorphosis") is used only four times—twice in reference to the transfiguration of Jesus, and twice in reference to the transformation of Christians. In Romans 12 Paul urges us not to be conformed to the world but to be transformed by the renewal of our minds in Christ. And in 2 Corinthians 3:18 he says that we, "beholding the glory of the Lord, are being changed [transformed] into his likeness from one degree of glory to another" (RSV). The transformation described, at least in these instances, cannot be applied to the social order as a whole. For the same reason I am not persuaded that there are sound theological grounds for speaking of the "conversion" of social structures.

To put this differently, the kingdom of God looks forward to the *ultimate* transformation of social structures, but in our broken, sinful world we are likely to make only small gains toward that goal. We are nevertheless called to work toward it, knowing that in Christ our present efforts and God's eternal purpose for us are linked, not separated. In the words of James Skillen, "Our attitude ought to be one of confidence that in Christ there is an intimate connection between this world and the coming kingdom, that there is no radical discontinuity between our labor in this world and our fulfillment in the next. But the coming kingdom is in God's hands not ours."[1]

I am arguing here for modest expectations regarding the social order—modest, that is, compared with utopian hopes. But for a hungry family, having food is not a modest improvement;

1. Skillen, "Christian Action and the Coming of Christ's Kingdom," in *Confessing Christ and Doing Politics,* ed. James Skillen (Washington: Association for Public Justice Education Fund, 1982), p. 89.

for the jobless, employment is not a modest improvement; for a family in which no one has had more than a fourth-grade education, seeing a child complete college is not a modest improvement; for a nation deeply in debt, saving millions or billions of dollars by rejecting an unneeded weapons system is not a modest improvement. These are all attainable goals. Focusing on attainable goals rather than on illusory visions is both politically and theologically sound. There are those who hold out the prospect of more dramatic social change than is warranted on either theological or empirical grounds. But let me hasten to add that the opposite tendency of expecting no social change worthy of our time and attention as Christians and therefore withdrawing from such concerns is a far more pervasive and regrettable stance. It interprets Jesus' pronouncement that "my kingdom is not of this world" to mean "this world is no concern of my kingdom," twisting his intent and disparaging a crucial opportunity for service.

What does all this mean with regard to hunger? There is no guarantee that hunger will be eliminated. It *can* be eliminated, just as slavery and tyranny have been eliminated in many places, so we must make every effort toward that end. But we have no reason to expect that gains against hunger will come easily. Such gains will be fiercely resisted by people who have a real or perceived interest in maintaining the status quo, and making them will require struggle every step of the way. This should come as no surprise to us. Nor should we use it as an excuse for doing nothing, as did the servant who buried the talent his master gave him. In Christ we are called to be the salt of the earth and a light to the world also in the public policy arena.

Compromise

Politics has been called "the art of the possible." Although this definition can be used as a convenient excuse for sacrificing one's convictions, it makes a valid point. In a democracy, politics is a vehicle for arriving at compromises among competing and sometimes conflicting interests. So if you want to accomplish things in public policy, you have to be willing to make reasonable compromises, because there are many competing interests and limited resources. Occasionally a clear and unambiguous victory will occur, but that is exceptional. Usually it's necessary to work on a "half a loaf" principle, and sometimes defend against setbacks. For example, 1984 legislation proposed by Bread for the World sought $50 million for a new Child Survival Fund. We got the fund established, but that year only $25 million was appropriated for it. On balance we considered it a significant gain. But this situation involved a fairly simple kind of compromise.

A different type of compromise occurs when there are competing values in the same legislation. For example, Bread for the World played an active role in one aspect of the tax reform package of 1986. As a hunger organization, we focused solely on the impact of taxation on low-income people. We did so because, while programs for assisting poor people had been severely cut during the early 1980s, their taxes were going up. That put them in a double bind and drove many of them more deeply into hunger and poverty. In 1978 a family of four living at the poverty line paid 4 percent of its income for federal taxes. By 1986 its tax burden had jumped to 11 percent of its income. These figures gave us a clear "fairness" case to present, and with it we generated considerable public support in favor of tax reform that would benefit poor people. As a result of our work and that of others, Congress included provisions that eliminated six million poor people from the income tax rolls. That eliminated a transfer of approximately $8 billion a year from the poor to the prosperous (the equivalent of $200,000 a year for each member of Bread for the World), and that will put more food on many tables. However, what made our support for the bill less than clear-cut was that it gave far more massive breaks to taxpayers in the very high income brackets—although it closed loopholes for wealthy taxpayers (and corporations) who were paying little or nothing to the IRS. But loopholes have a way of reappearing. That meant legislation with mixed results and long-term consequences that are not entirely clear.

Compromise usually begins before legislation is even introduced. When Bread for the World suggests legislation, we develop a proposal or a combination of proposals and test them with some members of Congress to see if the proposals have a reasonable chance of being considered in their present form or in what form they might obtain consideration. Legislation has to be introduced by members of Congress, who are seldom eager to sponsor bills that have no chance of passing. Bread for the World has developed a reputation among most members of Congress as a group that supports practical measures that can attract bipartisan support in Congress and among the public. Our approach is to move a step at a time. We would lose effectiveness if we began demanding legislation that few members of Congress would take seriously. Occasionally it is best to fight for a principle by proposing legislation that is certain to be defeated. But because the public policy process inescapably involves the art of the possible, unwillingness to compromise usually means getting nothing done—clearly an unsatisfactory path when the stakes are so high in terms of human lives.

Sometimes Bread for the World is urged to become more prophetic—that is, to campaign for government actions that will clearly not be taken, and do so in order to make a moral statement, to witness to what our nation should be doing. But there is a precariously fine line between being prophetic and being self-righteous. It is easy to indulge in a more-committed-than-thou stance without sufficient regard for the people on whose behalf we claim to struggle. Sometimes, I fear, the admonition to be prophetic masks despair on the part of those who have already given up hope of accomplishing much. Unwillingness to do good because "good" is not "best" may feel prophetic, but that is false consolation. The desire to be prophetic may reflect zeal that is not ready to deal with an imperfect world—but zeal can lead to cynicism when inflated hopes are dashed.

On the other hand, prophetic voices are needed, and true prophetic voices reflect what I call—for lack of a better term—a special vocation. I am convinced that some people are called to campaign for courses of action that are right even if they are not politically feasible. This is risky, because it may simply engage time, energy, and resources that could much more usefully be channeled elsewhere. On the other hand, such campaigning serves to remind us how far short we are of the ideal, and occasionally that plows the ground for some future harvest. But this vocation is seldom appropriate for a policy group that can achieve substantial gains by practicing the art of the possible. In any case, when we are seized by a prophetic mood, we would do well to stop and ask ourselves a hard question: Are we helping others, or are we shoring up our own need to feel morally superior?

Hunger and Wholeness

When we work to reduce hunger, we are dealing not with the full range or depth of human needs but only with one extreme need. If tomorrow we could bring about a world without hunger or even a world that met basic physical needs, we would still be surrounded by spiritual poverty. Put another way, food for the body does not provide food for the soul. Gandhi once observed, "To a hungry man, God comes in the form of bread." But to those who see Jesus as the Bread of Life, the meeting of physical needs falls far short of human wholeness.

This is the truth behind the untruth that it is therefore the calling of Christians to concentrate solely on the spiritual and eternal rather than the temporal welfare of others. This position is seriously flawed, first of all because those who espouse it have usually provided well for their *own* temporal needs, so what they are really willing to sacrifice are the temporal needs of others. Such a view also denies that it is the nature of God's love at work in us to reach out to those in physical as well as spiritual distress. To withhold love is to dishonor God, discredit our witness to Christ, and invite others to look elsewhere for salvation. By the same token, nothing so prepares people to believe in Christ as genuine evidence of love given with no strings attached. So while we recognize the limited nature of the goal of overcoming hunger and should not confuse physical well-being with spiritual wholeness, we can also recognize work toward that goal as a powerful sign of the kingdom. Christians who relate to people abroad only by supporting missionaries might well consider this point, because frequently the missionary enterprise is undermined by lack of evidence that the church cares when people are being exploited and oppressed.

Some might champion the spiritual over the temporal by saying that evangelism is more important than working for social justice. But that is a bit like saying that blood is more important than muscles in the body. In fact, each is important to the other, and both are essential for the well-being of the body. Changing the imagery, one could say that preaching the gospel is more important than family life. No doubt in a certain sense this is also true, and it is the reason why some have chosen to remain unmarried for the sake of the kingdom. But it is important to realize that preaching the gospel and family life are not competing opposites, and any attempt to disparage family responsibilities on the grounds that the other is more important undermines the credibility of the gospel. God has placed us in the world and surrounded us with responsibilities, and we are to lend authenticity to the gospel by the way in which we live our lives here. At stake is not only the wholeness of others but our own wholeness as well. We cannot withhold love and justice from others without doing injury to ourselves and retarding or otherwise jeopardizing our own spiritual growth.

Uncertainty

In Chapter Four I discussed the fact that Christians have foundational values to guide them but no special access to truth when it comes to policy prescriptions. So when we move from basic principles of faith to derived moral principles and then to specific policy positions, we expose ourselves increasingly to the possibility of misjudgment and error. Public policy is a complex, untidy business—but so is junior high school, so is farming, and so is marriage. Fortunately, we do not have to figure everything out by ourselves. On many issues we can lean on the analysis of others and the witness of the church. We can discuss issues with others. And we can draw on the resources of faith in the process. None of this relieves us of personal responsibility for the choices we make or the actions we take, but it does mean that we are not alone. In addition, struggling honestly through the uncertainties in this area can yield unexpected benefits, spurring our own growth and increasing our patience and understanding of those who may disagree with us.

Respect for the Choices of Others

One of the hazards of becoming citizen advocates is that we want everyone else to agree with us. The more deeply we get into an issue and the more emotionally involved we become, the more that desire grows. We not only think others should

agree with us, but we want them to actively support the same
cause. The temptation then arises to feel hurt, impatient, frus-
trated, or angry when they don't. These feelings add nothing to
our effectiveness or personal well-being, and they reflect a lack
of consideration for others. In our fervor for causes, it might
help us to remember the following things:

1. *Many people are barely able to cope with life's demands.*
Personal, family, or job-related problems may be more than they
can handle. Perhaps their faith and participation in church are
enabling them to hang on, but just barely, and for them that
may be a heroic achievement. They don't have the energy or the
disposition to think about taking part in a public policy campaign. It is not always obvious who these people are because on
the surface they may seem serene. We need to accept the fact
that people who fit this description will not be responsive to
our approaches, and they in turn need to feel that our trying to
enlist their aid is a gesture of love, not judgment.

2. *Not everyone feels called to serve through public policy issues.* A great many people who do not feel called to do so *should*.
But for a variety of reasons, some people serve better in other
ways. We need to respect that. An outstanding example is Mother
Teresa, who has devoted her life to assisting some of the poorest
of the poor—people left to die on the street, lepers, abandoned
children. A few years ago I visited several of her centers in and
around Calcutta. It is truly a humbling experience to see evidence of such love. None of this surprised me, however. What
did surprise me was my visit with the director of the Calcutta
Development Authority, who gave me a series of ads that the
CDA had been running in the newspapers that encouraged citizens to take pride in Calcutta and make it a better city. Two of
the ads singled out Mother Teresa as an example of someone
who didn't give up, who in the face of seeming hopelessness
was willing to take action. Her work, the CDA said, had a profound effect on the city by dispelling a sense of fatalism and
motivating others to help.

It is important for us to remember that in smaller ways many
people make an important but unsung contribution to the well-
being of society simply by being faithful parents or in other
ways reaching out in love to their fellowman. They may never
take up our public policy cause (although we should never as-

sume they will not), but they are faithfully loving and serving others in obedience to Christ, and in the process contributing more than most to a healthier world.

3. *Many issues need our consideration, but we can give time only to one or a few.* Of the multitude of policy issues—the environment, child abuse, the arms race, and a host of others—some are more important than others, and each deserves a participating public. But we have to make choices. We cannot be involved in them all. Everyone who enters the policy arena faces the same dilemma, and fortunately, not everyone chooses the same issue. I am inclined to think that everybody should make hunger his or her primary issue of concern. But the fact is that not everybody does or should do so. The issue someone else chooses may or may not be as important as hunger, but it may be an issue that he or she can better serve. I need to understand and respect that fact.

4. *Not everyone who takes up our issue will agree with us.* Some may work against our position. We have to allow for the possibility, however unpleasant and remote it may seem to us, that they may be right or at least partly right, and that in any case their motivation may be as good as ours. And even if none of the above is true (though we are seldom in a position to know), they still deserve our love and respect. This is an attitude that doesn't come naturally or easily to us, but it is the right attitude, because the means we employ must be consistent with the ends we seek.

The limitations I have sketched should not discourage us. On the contrary, awareness of them should help us move into policy issues with our eyes wide open, stripped of illusions that may lead to disappointment and early abandonment of a vital Christian ministry. If we can face these limitations constructively, we can contribute in an important way to the lives of others.

Chapter 8
You Can Make a Difference

The only thing necessary for the triumph of evil is for good men to do nothing.

—Anonymous

The sin of respectable people reveals itself in flight from responsibility.

—Eberhard Bethge

The decentralized nature of [our] political system, combined with the all-too-prevalent apathy of the public, produces a situation where people willing to be involved can soon have a greater influence than they ever expected to have.
—Stephen V. Monsma, *Pursuing Justice in a Sinful World*

Feeling Immobilized

"One person dying of hunger is a tragedy. A million people dying of hunger is a statistic," said Senator Mark Hatfield at a Bread for the World conference.

Hatfield had vividly pinpointed an underlying problem of the hunger issue. The hunger of a lone individual or a single family touches our hearts, and we instinctively find a way to reach out. But if the hunger of one person becomes the hunger of a million—or, as in the case of world hunger, literally hundreds of millions—we feel overwhelmed. We don't know what to do or even where to begin, so we may throw up our hands and say to ourselves, "What I do won't make any difference." Perhaps in self-defense we screen hunger out of our minds and walk away.

This "screening out" process struck home for me a few years ago when I watched a fascinating TV documentary called "Kitty: Return to Auschwitz." The program centered on a Jewish woman, Kitty Hart (now living in England) who during World War II survived the notorious Nazi concentration camp at Auschwitz, where tens of thousands of Jews were exterminated. As the television cameras followed her, Hart revisited Auschwitz with her son, a young physician, and told him step-by-step how she had managed to survive for two years as a teenager in that camp. Hart described one scene of horror after another. Eventually she came to the building where she had spent her last months in the camp, and she explained how hundreds of people had been marched by each day to their deaths. "But," she said (as I recall her explanation), "we didn't know. We knew, but we made ourselves not know, because knowing was more than you could bear. So you made yourself not know in order to keep going. It was only when an individual act of violence occurred, such as a child's being torn from its mother's arms and killed, that you were suddenly forced to realize what was happening."

That often describes our situation with regard to hunger as well as other issues and areas of life. We know, but we make ourselves not know because these realities are emotionally difficult to deal with. Hunger lends itself to that defense mechanism because few of us have contact with hungry people in our everyday world, so it is easy to think of hunger and hungry people as not quite real. We can walk away from them or simply keep hunger at a safe distance by reducing these people to statistics. And we can do the same thing with numerous other painful realities—victims of war, crime, discrimination, the federal deficit.

For this reason we do well to remind ourselves constantly that when we talk about such issues we are talking about real human beings. What may seem like an abstract problem to us is a life-or-death struggle for others. Like the statistics that go with them, the very terms "problem" and "issue" allow us to think impersonally about hunger or unemployment. We easily forget that the "issue" represents *people* whose lives are no less precious to God than your life or mine, or the lives of our children. That is where we must begin.

If the sheer magnitude of need does not immobilize us, guilt may. Guilt is a poor motivator. Few of us will tolerate for a sustained period of time the discomfort of feeling guilty about something we can easily avoid, so our inclination is to put out of mind the source of that discomfort. Again, a screening-out process occurs. We may feel guilty because we enjoy material abundance while others lack bare essentials or because we aren't doing much to help them. The late Rabbi Abraham Heschel often said (regarding the Vietnam war), "Some are guilty; all are responsible." Of course, if we are responsible and fail to respond, we are guilty, so the feeling of guilt may be well founded.

To see guilt as a poor motivator may help us look elsewhere for motivation. Appropriately so, for people of God live by grace. Guilt immobilizes us because it underscores our captivity to sin. But grace—God's undeserved love—sets us free to serve others. To live by grace means not to deny guilt but to live in the freedom of forgiveness. Because the message of the cross tells us that grace is not cheap but given at great cost to and with great love by the Giver, the only genuine response to it is profound gratitude that expresses itself in love to others. It is as forgiven sinners that we follow the example of Jesus by serving others— in the public policy arena as well as elsewhere.

Apathy also plays a part in our lack of response, and to the extent that it does, it reflects emptiness and shallowness of purpose. Apathy is not just the problem of others. It is a part of the human condition that each of us struggles with, and it is evidence that God's work in us is far from complete. Grace, not guilt, can help us overcome it.

Taking Action

It is important to understand with unmistakable clarity that we are not helpless. Our action can make a significant difference. We can let our opinions be known to those who decide policy for the state or the nation, and we can do so in a timely, effective manner.

Let me stress again that a public policy response is not the only one we can make. We can also pray. David Beckmann, an economist at the World Bank, once wrote in a memo to me, "If Christians would routinely remember the poor in their personal and corporate prayers, a lot would follow. So first get your prayers right." Along with our prayers we can offer direct assistance. (Where hunger is concerned, that may mean contributing to private agencies or helping out at a local soup kitchen or food pantry.) We can learn more about an issue, discuss it with our family and friends, get a group started in church for study and action, and much more. Each of these efforts is highly important.

The response I focus on in this book, however, is that of influencing decisions regarding government policies. I do so because I have seen that making other essential responses to human need while neglecting public policy is often a formula for failure. We don't need to be part of that formula. Through the process of national as well as state and local decision-making, we can work for a more just world at home and abroad. Seeking justice is often the best way—and sometimes the only way beyond prayer—of loving people in need who are otherwise beyond our reach. But it can be a tellingly effective way of doing so.

A few years ago a group called the Kentucky Fair Tax Coalition successfully challenged a law that allowed the owners of mineral rights to destroy land surfaces in Kentucky in order to mine coal. The legality of the "broad form" deed that permitted such damage was struck down in the courts. Citizen action changed public policy and benefited many people. This same group succeeded in getting a county tax levied on coal so that some of the wealth it was producing for others stayed in the counties from which it came. This in turn meant revenues to meet public and social needs in economically depressed coal counties.

Or take the example of a fourteen-member task force in Delaware. From 1975 to 1985, Delaware's prison population multiplied more than fivefold, overcrowding the prisons. So the state formed a commission to develop alternatives to imprisonment for less serious offenders. At the same time, a newly formed Justice Fellowship task force began to contact judges around the state and create a positive public climate for the commission's work. The task force also played a role in getting the state legislature to appropriate money for an alternative sentencing program and helped form a group to match offenders with businesses that would employ them until they had paid back their victims. Tom Quinn, executive director of Delaware's Criminal Justice Council, said of the task force members, "They have stayed right on top of our sentencing reform efforts. Because they have expressed their views to their elected representatives, the legislators know that there are people who want a more productive response to crime."

Expressing our views is important. Based on his experience in Congress, my brother Paul says, "One letter to a member of Congress on a hunger issue saves a life." That may sound like an exaggeration, but Bread for the World's experience is that, if anything, Paul has understated the case. Of course, it's not possible to trace each letter to a particular life that has been saved. And on most policy issues for which favorable action is obtained it is difficult to come up with even a rough estimate of how many people have benefited. For example, Bread for the World's efforts with regard to the African famine helped bring about a substantially greater response from the United States than would otherwise have been made. It is impossible to say how much greater the response was and how many thousands of lives were saved as a result, but clearly we are talking about huge numbers.

In 1981 Bread for the World played a key role in getting Congress to establish a four-million-ton emergency wheat reserve. In 1985 the Administration tapped that reserve in order to channel an additional 300,000 tons of grain to African countries, enough to supply a daily ration of more than a pound of grain to ten million people for sixty days. How many people were thus spared from disease, disability, or death? We have no way of counting, though the numbers are large.

The impact of most legislative gains is even harder to measure, although the effect may be extensive. But let me tell you the story of one achievement that does lend itself to measurement: the Child Survival Fund.

The Child Survival Fund was part of a package of measures that Bread for the World helped to develop as the Human Needs and World Security Bill of 1984. Congress established the Child Survival Fund and appropriated $25 million for it in 1985. This was increased to $37.5 million in 1986 and $75 million in 1987—an amount triple that of the initial appropriation. The purpose of the Child Survival Fund is to channel money to various agencies that use it exclusively for the purpose of promoting four simple health practices that dramatically reduce the death rate among young children in developing countries. (The four practices are oral rehydration, breast-feeding, the use of growth charts, and immunization.)

UNICEF has been in the forefront of recent efforts to promote these practices, which hold out the prospect of preventing half of the more than 40,000 deaths of young children that occur each day, and of doing so in less than a decade. James P. Grant, executive director of UNICEF, told me that for every hundred dollars that agency spends on direct health-related aid to children of the very poor, a child's life is saved—quite apart from other health benefits. If we apply that formula (a life saved for every hundred dollars spent), 750,000 children will live rather than die as the result of just one year's funding of the Child Survival Fund—that's three quarters of a million lives. If we divide this number by Bread for the World's total membership, the result is *almost twenty children "saved" by each member of Bread for the World;* without their letters of support to Congress, the Child Survival Fund would never have been started. As each year brings additional appropriations for the Child Survival Fund, and as U.S. contributions prompt other donor countries to contribute more for this health revolution, the number of children whose lives are spared will multiply.

The proposal for a Child Survival Fund was part of a larger effort to increase U.S. assistance for basic health services in poor countries. The increase that occurred triggered a study that was funded by the National Science Foundation and completed by two faculty members from Johns Hopkins University, who reported the following in the *American Journal of Public Health:*

> Historically, the Agency for International Development (AID) health budget has been closely tied to overall development spending. A large increase in the international health appropriations in 1984 broke this pattern. Investigation shows that active grassroots organizing and congressional lobbying are the most likely responsible factors in the increase. . . .
>
> Examination of the events leading to this extraordinary increase in international health funding revealed the central organizing role played by a non-denominational Christian interest group called Bread for the World.[1]

1. John O. Quinley and Timothy Baker, "Lobbying for International Health: The Link Between Good Ideas and Funded Programs—Bread for the World and the Agency for International Development," *American Journal of Public Health,* July 1986, pp. 793-96.

The report concluded that those interested in promoting international public health would do well to participate in the kind of citizen advocacy that brought about this increase.

Another example of effective advocacy in the area of public health is the work of the Children's Defense Fund. The same year that Congress set up the Child Survival Fund, it also approved legislation to extend health coverage in this country to an additional half million poor children as well as to a smaller number of pregnant women. This was the first time in the two decades since Medicaid had been established that eligibility had been significantly increased for women and children. Although several million poor children remain uncovered by either public or private health insurance, this legislation was an important achievement, and it happened to a large extent through the efforts of the Children's Defense Fund. The following year the Children's Defense Fund took the lead in developing legislation and establishing a coalition of groups in Texas that brought about reforms to improve health care services for 300,000 poor children and adults in that state. In combination these policy actions directly benefited almost one million poor people.

The bottom line, then, is that you can make a difference. Your life can count, and count importantly, for others. I have been illustrating this point primarily with the issue of hunger because it is the one I know best. But the point applies to many public justice issues. You can help. You don't have to walk away from people. Through public policy efforts you can become engaged in a truly life-saving, life-benefiting ministry.

How Advocacy Works

I wish you could be in my shoes and observe the changes that take place when Bread for the World members contact their U.S. senators and representatives. You would see for yourself the importance of serving as a citizen advocate. Doing so does not take a great deal of time, but it does take some. And it takes a willingness to follow issues in our newsletter and write an occasional letter—a simple, straightforward letter expressing your views in your own words. That may seem too small and ordinary a task to amount to much, but then the really important agents of change in life often seem that way: words, water, bread and wine, for starters. Or perhaps citizen lobbying seems to require too much time in an already overcrowded personal schedule. But in what other way can you do so much with your life for so modest an investment?

Let me give you a few examples.

In the summer of 1980, emergency food aid was desperately needed to deal with a worsening famine in Somalia and a still-critical food shortage in Cambodia. But the House Appropriations Committee turned down a request from the Administration for money to pay for that aid. With a vote by the full House of Representatives coming up the following week, chances of reversing the Committee's decision seemed slim because the Administration had withdrawn its support for additional funds. Yet the situation in those countries was critical. Bread for the World policy analyst Ernest Loevinsohn met with Representative Floyd Fithian (D-Ind.), and the two developed the following strategy. On the floor of the House, Fithian would introduce an amendment to the Committee's legislation. The amendment would cut $100 million from government spending on furniture while restoring $43 million of that amount for emergency food aid. Our hope was to attract votes from those who wanted increased food aid and/or wanted to trim government spending. Meanwhile, those serving on the Bread for the World telephone networks ("quicklines") in congressional districts throughout the country got the word out to our members within a few days, asking them to phone or wire their representatives in support of Fithian's amendment. The strategy worked. The amendment won by a large majority. Later an official from the U.S. Agency for International Development told me, "Every penny of that $43 million was needed to fend off starvation, especially in Somalia."

Occasionally we ask our entire membership to write, call, wire, or visit their senators or their representatives when a vote on an important bill is coming up before the full House or Senate. Usually we know well ahead of time when this is going to happen, and we can get word to our members through a monthly newsletter. In that case our quicklines are put into operation only in areas where senators or representatives may be undecided. Sometimes the legislation is hotly debated and close, so each vote—and each letter or phone call from one of our members—could change the outcome. In 1982 the House vote to require that more U.S. aid be targeted to benefit the very poor passed by a 227 to 184 margin, but the outcome was in doubt right up until the roll call. In 1984 the vote to prevent further increases in military and security aid to developing countries was defeated in the House by the most frustrating of margins— 208 to 207.

We also aim at the entire House or Senate when we are helping to launch a new piece of major legislation. A large number of co-sponsors indicates widespread interest in the bill and makes committee action more likely. Because only a small percentage of the huge number of bills introduced each year gets serious consideration, strong support at the outset helps. It was therefore a welcome surprise when, in 1984, after intensive work by Bread for the World members in North Carolina, Senator Jesse Helms (R-N.C.) signed on as a co-sponsor of a bill providing emergency aid to Africa. Helms almost always opposes measures sought by Bread for the World, so his support in this instance was a significant gain, especially since we needed rapid action.

More than 90 percent of all legislation dies in committee,[2] so some of our most intensive work is focused at that level. We pinpoint districts or states represented by members of a House or Senate committee or subcommittee, and Bread for the World members in those areas "lobby" their senators or representatives to obtain action. In 1982 we needed to have Representative Paul Findley (R-Ill.) take a leadership role in the House Foreign Affairs Committee on a proposal that would encourage the development of food reserves at the village level in Africa. Findley wavered. We used one of several quicklines in Findley's district to generate letters to him. Later Findley's aide told our staff that Findley had gotten "a ton of mail" on the issue. Asked how many letters had actually been received, the aide replied, "Twenty." (That works out to about a hundred pounds per letter.) The provision passed in the committee, in large part because Findley effectively pushed for it there. Unfortunately, we do not always achieve the policy goals we seek, and in this

2. According to the Congressional Research Service, approximately 10,000 bills were introduced in the 97th Congress (1981-82). Of these, 855 reached the floor for a vote, and 473 of them became public law.

instance, despite committee approval, Congress subsequently failed to enact the measure.

We faced a similar situation in the Senate regarding a targeted proposal for development aid, which required that at least 40 percent of U.S. development aid directly benefit the very poor. In this instance we considered the support of Senator Richard Lugar (R-Ind.) essential, since he was a key Republican on the Senate Foreign Relations Committee, where the legislation was stalled. We had reason to believe that Lugar's support could turn the tide in that committee. But Lugar, a Republican, faced strong opposition from the Reagan Administration. So our Indiana members wrote letters to Lugar. They also arranged to have a letter submitted to the *Indianapolis Star* by prominent church leaders from around the state urging Lugar's support. In addition, a few Bread for the World members from Indiana met with Senator Lugar's legislative director. Not long afterward, Tom Hunsdorfer, our Indiana state coordinator, received a letter from Lugar's legislative director confirming that Senator Lugar had decided to co-sponsor the bill. "Your own efforts and those of other Hoosiers were instrumental in his decision," the director pointed out. Senator Lugar's support opened the way for a favorable vote in the Senate Foreign Relations Committee, which was an essential step in getting the entire Congress to pass the measure.

As you may gather from these examples, it is one thing to line up a favorable vote by a member of Congress. It is quite another to obtain leadership from busy legislators, who have to choose only a few issues among many for their special efforts. Yet without good leadership, no favorable action occurs. So it is no small request to ask a senator or a representative to take the lead on a particular piece of legislation.

Simply asking for a favorable vote is no small request, either, but it should not be viewed as an imposition. When Bread for the World members lobby for a bill, they call attention to a matter of considerable importance that might otherwise go unnoticed, and they provide members of Congress with information on it, thus performing a valuable service for these elected officials, not to mention for hungry people.

If the stories I have recounted here make you think, "Bread for the World is working well. No need for me to join," that would be a great mistake—another yielding to the "what I do won't make any difference" syndrome. Bread for the World has won some battles, but we have also lost some because we couldn't muster a strong enough showing of public support. And our country is still far from making the demise of hunger a major domestic or foreign policy objective. An enormous amount of work remains to be done because immense numbers of people remain hungry. What Bread for the World can hope to accomplish is directly related to our size—to the number of members we have who communicate their opinions in a timely fashion to the decision-makers. The more people we have taking part in this work, the more we can accomplish.

Nurturing Hope

To look at world hunger or some other crucial human problem and to say "What I do won't make any difference" is wrong not only because it contradicts clear evidence, but more fundamentally because it is the counsel of despair, and despair is unbelief. However, we are people of faith and hope, not people of despair. Our hope is rooted not in statistical trends or the prospect of technological breakthroughs that promise an end to injustice, but in the God who raised Jesus from death to life. As the apostle Peter put it, "Blessed be the God and Father of our Lord Jesus Christ! By his great mercy we have been born anew to a living hope through the resurrection of Jesus Christ from the dead" (1 Pet. 1:3, RSV). We are people of hope, born anew to follow Jesus' example by living for others. That hope sustains us for the struggle, regardless of economic or political developments and long after others have tired of the challenge and turned to other pursuits.

There is also a less ultimate hope, of course, the kind people are referring to when they ask me, "What hope do you see for progress against hunger?" On this level the signs are mixed, and assurances elude us. Hunger *can* be eliminated. *But what will happen depends on the choices we make.* That's why the commitment of each one of us is so vitally important. None of us can control the choices of others, but each of us can control his or her own choice. If you choose to work for policies that help reduce hunger, your efforts will make a difference. They will not guarantee the reduction of hunger worldwide (though they make that outcome more likely), but they will make a difference in the lives of others, and that is promise enough. Whatever we do that is consistent with God's intention yields a harvest. Like the Word of God, such deeds do not return empty. We may seldom be able to measure the results with any precision, but our efforts will not be wasted. This is true even when our best attempts seem to result in failure, because what God requires of us is not success but faithfulness. God will attend to the outcome.

When God calls us to stand with brothers and sisters who are hungry (or are sick or in prison or in some other distress), he is not saddling us with some onerous task. He is not cheating us of life, taking something away from us. On the contrary, he is inviting us to celebrate the kingdom more fully—to enjoy life more deeply and completely. That is the marvel of God's purpose for us. It is the paradox of the kingdom: "Whoever would save his life will lose it; and whoever loses his life for my sake and the gospel's will save it" (Mark 8:35, RSV).

Many years ago I remember hearing Indian evangelist D. T. Niles speak on John 3:16. He pointed out that Christians are twice-converted people. They are first converted from the world to Jesus Christ, Niles said. But then they are converted to the world again, to love the world and relate to it, not as they did before but through the heart and mind of Christ. I think of serving by shaping public policies as part of our second conversion: our call each day to die to worldliness and to love the world with the heart and mind of Christ.

In the case of hunger and many other crucial human concerns, the need for twice-converted Christians has never been greater.

The love of God and the need of others bear witness.

Appendix I
How to Contact Members of Congress

Address:

The Hon. (Name)
U.S. Senate
Washington, D.C. 20510

The Hon. (Name)
U.S. House of Representatives
Washington, D.C. 20515

Phone for House and Senate offices in Washington:
(202) 224-3121

United States senators and representatives also have offices in their states or districts, and you can call or meet with a staff member there. Your municipal or county office will be able to give you further information.

Letters

There is nothing especially difficult about writing to your U.S. senators or representative (or other leaders in government). Here are a few practical suggestions:

1. Make your letter brief and clear. Say what you have to say in a few sentences. Elaborate only if you need to explain an issue.

2. Be courteous. Remember that the person you are writing to is human and deserves to be approached in a loving, considerate manner, even if you disagree on an issue. Letters that scold and sound cranky do more damage than good.

3. Remember that it doesn't matter whether your letter is typed or handwritten.

4. Avoid form letters. They are seldom effective. Use your own words.

5. Be specific. A letter urging a member of Congress to "do something about hunger" usually doesn't help much. Instead, address a particular piece of legislation if you can. Example:

> Dear Congressman Smith:
>   I am writing to ask you to become a sponsor of "The Human Needs and World Security Act" introduced by Representative Tony Hall. This bill is important because . . .

6. Be timely. Write when a bill is being considered. To be timely and specific on an issue, you often need to get information from an organization that specializes in that issue.

If the reply you receive is a form letter, that may be good news. It may indicate that the senator or representative is receiving enough letters on the issue to have drafted a standard reply.

Phone Calls

Phone calls may be as effective as or even more effective than letters, though usually calls are made either because you need to explain something or because time is short and a vote is coming up within a day or two. You will usually talk to a staff member who handles that particular issue. Be courteous, clear, and get to the point. If you are calling Washington, D.C., remember the time zones. For example, 6:00 A.M. in California is 9:00 A.M. in D.C. That is worth remembering, because you won't have much competition from other Californians at 6:00 A.M., and the call is much less expensive than it would be during prime calling hours.

Telegrams and Mailgrams

Telegrams are also effective and fast. If you can express your message in twenty words or less, send a personal opinion message; it's cheaper than a regular telegram, and offers same-day delivery. Mailgrams also cost less than telegrams (though a bit more than personal opinion messages). They allow a message of up to fifty words, but they are delivered the next day.

Meetings

Best of all, when you can arrange it, is a meeting. You should call well in advance to arrange a time and a place. If you ask the member of Congress to specify when he/she is available for such contact, you have a better chance of scheduling a meeting. It is usually easier for your U.S. representative than for one of your two U.S. senators to arrange a meeting. Often representatives travel around the state or district from time to time and make themselves available during announced hours. They may also hold town meetings where you can ask them questions about your issue. Still better, invite the member of Congress to speak at your church some evening on the issue you are concerned about, or ask him/her simply to meet with a group to discuss the issue informally. Such meetings can be effective in arousing interest and support for (or against) a position and can lead to ongoing contact with that person or his/her staff. Keep in mind that meeting with the right staff aide is also an effective way of delivering a message and sometimes easier to arrange.

Courtesy is always important. You have something to contribute, but you also have something to learn. Prepare in advance what you want to say, and try to anticipate the possible arguments against your position and how you can respond to them.

Remember that meetings often lay the groundwork for ongoing contact with a congressional office.

Appendix II
The Right-to-Food Resolution

Passed by the United States Senate*
(Senate Concurrent Resolution 138)
by voice vote on
September 16, 1976

WHEREAS in this Bicentennial Year we reaffirm our national commitment to the inalienable right of all to life, liberty, and the pursuit of happiness, none of which can be realized without food to adequately sustain and nourish life, and we recall that the right to food and freedom from hunger was set forth in the Universal Declaration of Human Rights and in the World Food Conference Declaration of 1974, and

WHEREAS the report entitled "The Assessment of the World Food Situation," prepared for the 1974 World Food Conference, estimated that four hundred and sixty million persons, almost half of them young children, are malnourished; and

WHEREAS nearly half of the human race lives on diets seriously deficient in proteins or other essential nutrients; and

WHEREAS most of this hunger and malnutrition is suffered by the poor in developing countries whose poverty prevents them from obtaining adequate food; and

WHEREAS the demand for food is accelerating and the unprecedented growth in population will add a billion persons to the world's population in less than 15 years; and

WHEREAS the Food and Agriculture Organization, and other recognized authorities, currently estimate that by 1985 the developing countries will experience an annual food deficit of 85 million tons; and

*Five days later, on September 21, 1976, the U.S. House of Representatives passed a similar resolution (House Concurrent Resolution 737) by a vote of 340 to 61.

WHEREAS it is in the interest of the United States and all nations to overcome food shortages which cause human suffering and generate economic and political instability; and

WHEREAS the United States proposed, and all nations at the World Conference of 1974 accepted, the bold objective "that within a decade no child will go to bed hungry, that no family will fear for its next day's bread, and that no human being's future and capacities will be stunted by malnutrition"; and

WHEREAS the international community has repeatedly urged the industrialized nations to increase their official development assistance to 0.7 percent of their total national production (GNP); and

WHEREAS the elimination of global hunger and malnutrition cannot succeed without expanded self-help efforts by the developing countries: Now, therefore, be it

RESOLVED by the House of Representatives (the Senate concurring), That it is the sense of Congress that

(1) the United States reaffirms the right of every person in this country and throughout the world to food and a nutritionally adequate diet; and

(2) the need to combat hunger shall be a fundamental point of reference in the formulation and implementation of United States policy in all areas which bear on hunger including international trade, monetary arrangements, and foreign assistance; and

(3) in the United States, we should seek to improve food assistance problems for all those who are in need, to ensure that all eligible recipients have the opportunity to receive a nutritionally adequate diet, and to reduce unemployment and ensure a level of economic decency for everyone; and

(4) the United States should emphasize and expand its assistance for self-help development among the world's poorest people, especially in countries seriously affected by hunger and malnutrition, with particular emphasis on increasing food production and encouraging more equitable patterns of food distribution and economic growth; and such assistance, in order to be effective, should be coordinated with expanded efforts by international organizations, donor nations, and the recipient countries to provide a nutritionally adequate diet for all.

Questions for Discussion

Chapter 1

1. What has been your personal journey regarding faith and public policy?

2. What dangers do you see facing Christians who take an active role in public policy matters? What opportunities do you see?

3. The author makes a sharp distinction between the separation of church and state, and the separation of religion from life. What are your thoughts on this?

Chapter 2

1. The biblical writers before the time of Christ addressed the problems of hunger and poverty. What strikes you as surprising or impressive about their witness?

2. What seems surprising or impressive about the witness concerning hunger and poverty in the New Testament?

3. What myths or misconceptions about hunger and poverty are most common? How are these related to our understanding of the Bible?

4. Why do the social and political environments of the Old and New Testament need to be taken into account as we relate the biblical witness to our own situation?

Chapter 3

1. The quotes at the beginning of the chapter have a common thread. What is it? Does it help us understand what our reponse to social injustice should be?

2. In your opinion, what is the most appropriate role for government to play regarding hunger (or another issue)?

3. If the Bible does not describe for us the most appropriate role for government on most issues, then what bearing, if any, does the Bible have on this matter?

4. Is the case that the author makes for government action persuasive? Why or why not?

Chapter 4

1. How do we determine God's will for us when we face difficult choices in life?

2. The author warns against direct leaps from the Bible or faith to specific policy prescriptions. What is the danger of making such a leap?

3. Is making such a leap a greater or a lesser danger than making no effort to let the Bible inform our thinking on policy matters?

4. Are you comfortable dealing with the uncertainty that the author says we should acknowledge when arriving at public policy positions?

5. What can we learn from this uncertainty? How can this help us and not immobilize us?

Chapter 5

1. What can we learn from history regarding an appropriate role for the church on matters of public policy?

2. The author says that "there are wise ways and foolish ways" for the church to deal with policy issues. What are some foolish ways? Some wise ways?

3. What is your response to the statement that "the church should preach the gospel and not get involved in politics"?

4. Discuss the pros and cons of official church statements on policy matters.

5. How could the ministry of Christians through public policy be enhanced in your congregation?

Chapter 6

1. Do you agree with the author's assessment of the new religious right?

2. Do you agree with the author that "the religious left can be just as thoroughly seduced by ideological or cultural sirens, just as prone to leap from faith to policy positions, and just as judgmental as the religious right"?

3. This chapter comes down hard on ideological approaches. Why? Is it possible and/or desirable to have no ideological bias?

4. What positive role can public policy groups play?

Chapter 7

1. Facing our limitations is always a humbling enterprise. How well do you handle this? Do you end up feeling discouraged or better equipped for action?

2. What are some of the limitations that you think are important to recognize as we deal with public policy issues?

3. Our view of human nature affects our expectations regarding social change. What position do you take in this discussion?

4. What is your opinion of the section in this chapter on "hunger and wholeness"?

5. How successful are you at respecting the choices of others?

Chapter 8

1. How widespread is the feeling that "what I do won't make any difference"?

2. How is this feeling related to Christian hope and faith?

3. Have you found effective ways to address this feeling in yourself? in others?

4. What action can you take and suggest that others take in the policy arena that can make a significant difference?

5. D. T. Niles is cited as saying that Christians are twice-converted people. Have we slighted the "second conversion"? If so, does that also slight our "first conversion"?

☐ I want to be an advocate and use my influence to shape national policies that help people who are poor and hungry.

Enclosed is my membership contribution of

☐ $100+   Sponsoring Member

☐ $ 50-$99   Contributing Member

☐ $ 25   Member (If $25 is a financial hardship, please give what you can.)

☐ Please bill me for the membership indicated above.

☐ Please send me more information about Bread for the World.

NAME _____

ADDRESS _____

CITY _____ STATE _____ ZIP _____

RELIGIOUS AFFILIATION _____

OCCUPATION _____

bread for the world
a christian citizens' movement in the usa

(202) 269-0200

802 rhode island avenue n.e. washington, d.c. 20018

BUSINESS REPLY MAIL

FIRST CLASS   PERMIT NO. 14174   WASHINGTON, D.C. 20066

POSTAGE WILL BE PAID BY ADDRESSEE

bread for the world

802 rhode island avenue. n.e.
washington, d.c. 20077-5204